EDITOR: LEE JOHN

 ELITE SER

CW00735803

WELLINGTON'S
FOOT GUARDS

Text by
IAN FLETCHER
Colour plates by
WILLIAM YOUNGHUSBAND

First published in 1994 by
Osprey, an imprint of Reed Consumer Books Limited
Michelin House, 81 Fulham Road,
London SW3 6RB
and Auckland, Melbourne, Singapore and Toronto

ISBN 1 85532 392 3

Filmset in Great Britain by Keyspools Ltd, Golborne,
Lancashire.
Printed through Bookbuilders Ltd, Hong Kong.

Author's note

This volume is designed to complement Men-at-Arms
114 and 119, both of which also deal with Wellington's
infantry. To avoid duplication the reader is directed to
these as they cover many aspects of the drill, training
and basic army life of Wellington's Foot Guards that
would otherwise be included herein. The emphasis in
this volume is firmly upon those aspects that made the
Foot Guards such a different body of fighting troops:
an élite.

Artist's Note

Readers may care to note that the original paintings
from which the colour plates in this book were
prepared are available for private sale. All
reproduction copyright whatsoever is retained by the
publisher. All enquiries should be addressed to:

William Younghusband
12 St Matthew's Walk
Chapel Allerton
Leeds LS7 3PS

The publishers regret that they can enter into no
correspondence upon this matter.

Acknowledgements

Thanks go to Major (Ret'd) P.A. Lewis, of RHQ
Grenadier Guards, for the Bridgeman cloak
photograph, and to Lieutenant-Colonel T.J. Tedder
for permission to reproduce it; to Lieutenant-General
The Hon. Sir William Rous, KCB OBE, for the
painting of John Rous and his shoulder belt plate and
shako plate; to Colonel Peter Walton of the Army
Museums Ogilby Trust. Thanks also to Gary Gibbs
and Bob Marrion for their help regarding sergeants'
greatcoats.

WELLINGTON'S FOOT GUARDS

INTRODUCTION

Every army has among its establishment a unit which is considered its élite. In the British Army under the Duke of Wellington one or two units, such as those of the Light Division, could lay claim to élite status on the basis of their records. But surely the élite troops of Wellington's army were the Foot Guards. On being asked a few years after Waterloo for his opinion as to the relative merits of the Foot Guards and the Line regiments of the British Army, Wellington said, 'Oh! I am all for the Guards – all for the Guards,' upon which the enquirer replied, 'Those fellows in silk stockings have more blood about them, and blood (i.e. breeding) will tell.' However, Wellington retorted that he meant the non-commissioned officers of

The 3rd Foot Guards at the Battle of Talavera, 28 July 1809. The bareheaded officer in the centre is Captain Robert Dalrymple, erroneously shown wearing an ensign's uniform, who was killed during the battle. The men wear loose white summer trousers and carry the black 'Trotter'-pattern knapsack. Note the sergeants with their spontoons around the colours. After a painting by Lawson.

the Guards as he rated these very highly indeed – proof of which can be found in the high number of Guards' NCOs he recommended for commissions in different regiments. The Duke paid one memorable compliment to the Guards' NCOs when he said that although they got drunk as much as anybody else in the army, they did at least see to it that their duties were carried out first.

The NCOs of the Guards were, of course, fiercely proud of their regiments' reputations as highly trained and disciplined soldiers, and new recruits were put through a strenuous period of training to ensure that this tradition was maintained: a tradition of unquestioning obedience, endurance, loyalty and, above all, regimental pride. It was not enough that their men were well turned out – they had to be absolutely immaculate, and this extended not only to their personal appearance but also to their equipment, weapons and quarters. Attention to detail was meticulous; after all, these were Royal Household troops, men who would be present on State occasions such as the Trooping of the Colour and who performed guard duties at St James's Palace and at Windsor.

On campaign, of course, standards were difficult to maintain but even here the Guards took care of their appearance. During the retreat to Corunna in 1809, for instance, the army as a whole was reduced to a shadow of that which had landed six months earlier. The Guards suffered as much as any regiment; but when the 28th Regiment were shuffling along the road during the retreat they found the 1st Foot Guards halted by the roadside, cleaning their equipment, much of which was hanging from trees to keep it out of the snow. Fortunately, a good proportion of recruits came to the Guards via the Militia, which meant that these men would have at least two years' experience of drill behind them before the NCOs of the Guards set about them with their own rigorous brand of training.

Ensign the Hon. John Edward Cornwallis Rous, later 2nd Earl of Stradbroke, in the uniform of the Coldstream Guards, 1810. After a painting by Thomas Beach. The shoulder belt plate and gorget worn by Rous in this painting are pictured elsewhere in this book.

That the NCOs of the Guards were extremely efficient cannot be denied; but it was the composition of the officer corps, the 'fellows in silk stockings', that gave the regiments of Foot Guards their real character. It was with good reason that the 1st Division of the army, in which the Guards were brigaded in the Peninsula, was nicknamed 'The Gentlemen's Sons'. This nickname referred to the high proportion of officers with aristocratic or land-owning backgrounds.

Probably the most oft-quoted reference to 'The Gentlemen's Sons' relates to an incident towards the end of the Peninsular War when the Guards were positioned near Bayonne in southern France. Wellington, accompanied by Lord Hill and Colonel Fre-

mantle of the Coldstream Guards, was passing a redoubt by the roadside. It was raining, and as Wellington looked up he was surprised to see many of the Guards officers holding umbrellas to keep off the rain. Shortly afterwards Lord Hill galloped over to them and said, 'Lord Wellington does not approve of the use of umbrellas during the enemy's firing, and will not allow the "gentlemen's sons" to make themselves ridiculous in the eyes of the army.' A few days later, Tynling received 'a wigging' from Wellington for allowing so many of his officers to carry umbrellas in the face of the enemy and added, 'The Guards may in uniform, when on duty at St James's, carry them if they please; but in the field it is not only ridiculous but unmilitary.' This episode says much of

The Hon. William Rufus Rous, younger brother of John Rous, wearing the uniform of the Light Company of the Coldstream Guards, c.1810. After a painting by Thomas Beach.

Major-General Warde, 1st Foot Guards, 1809, after an engraving by J. Gurdee, 1809. Warde commanded the Brigade of Guards in the Peninsula in 1808. In the background are an officer, sergeant and privates of the Grenadier Company, 1st Foot Guards. Although bearskins were worn only for State occasions they were, evidently, taken on campaign; archives of the 1st Foot Guards show that their grenadiers at Barrosa had both ordinary caps and bearskins.

bankers and lawyers). Indeed, if one includes those serving on the Staff, this élite body of officers at Waterloo included seven peers, 25 sons or heirs of peers, five knights, nine sons or heirs of baronets, and one son of a knight. Of all the titled officers serving in the British Army at the outbreak of the Peninsular War, nearly a third could be found in the three regiments of Foot Guards.

Such were the high purchase prices of commissions that only the well-connected or titled could afford to join this socially exclusive military caste. Even when the young officer had bought his colours he would need a further sum of money to meet the expenses incurred in order for him to live in the style and manner expected of the Foot Guards both at home and, wherever possible, on campaign. Comparisons of the prices of commissions and rates of pay in 1815 between the Guards and the Line regiments are worthy of note. In the Guards, a lieutenant-colonelcy cost £6,700, a majority £6,300, a captaincy £3,500 and a lieutenancy £1,500. The equivalent ranks in the Line regiments would cost £3,500, £2,600, £1,500 and £550 respectively. With regard to pay, a major in

the Guards officer's philosophy towards campaigning and their ability to make the best of a bad situation – passing it off in as comfortable a manner as possible.

The Officers Corps

When the rest of Wellington's army dubbed the Guards Brigades of the 1st Division 'The Gentlemen's Sons' they were not far from the truth. When it came to the composition of the officer corps the Guards were unrivalled. They came only from the higher echelons of society, from the aristocracy and landed gentry and from the families of successful merchants and tradesmen (the term 'tradesmen' referring not to the commercial class, as is today's meaning, but to wealthy professional men such as

the Guards received £1 4s 6d per day, a captain 16s 6d, and a lieutenant 7s 10d; their equivalents in the Line regiments received 16s, 10s 6d, and 6s 6d per day.

The regiments of Foot Guards were, therefore, for the affluent only. Moreover, an officer of the Guards would expect to pay not only for his service dress but also for elaborate state uniforms, worn to the various functions held at Windsor or St James's and on state occasions such as the Trooping of the Colour. On top of these costs they could also expect to pay even more towards mess bills during the course of a year – the Guards officers often dining in lavish fashion; all of this necessitated a considerable private income. Those fashionable haunts of the rich, famous and powerful, London's gentlemen's clubs, became meeting places for the Guards; among the most prominent were White's, Boodle's, Brookes's, Arthur's and Graham's. Here the Guards mixed with politicians and socialites, indulging in various card games such as whist, faro and macao; fortunes could be won and lost at the table – the Duke of Portland's father-in-law, General Scott, won the vast sum of £200,000 at whist. These clubs were concentrated in the west end of London, mainly in the Piccadilly area, and entry into White's in particular was very difficult indeed. Most of the nobility were members, and it says much that officers of the Guards were accepted. They also had their own club, the Guards Club. This was run along military lines, and the only games played were billiards and low whist; Gronow claimed

The 1st Foot Guards embark at Ramsgate for the Peninsula in September 1808, after a painting by De Loutherbourg. A variety of legwear can be seen in this painting: blue trousers worn by the sergeant, white breeches with black gaiters, and loose white overalls buttoned up the side. The men's packs are brown canvas and bear the regimental star.

Captain Robert Dalrymple, 3rd Foot Guards, painted in an ensign's undress uniform. After a painting by Angelica Kauffmann.

led army arrived in a sorry state as the pursuing French army closed in on them; but as he and his staff watched the British troops begin to arrive they were astonished to see one particular unit come marching over the hill in parade step, the sergeants keeping an eye on the men's dressing while the drum major twirled his baton around him. Moore turned to Sir Robert Anstruther and said simply, 'Look at that body of men in the distance; they are the Guards, by the way they are marching.' This is probably the most famous quote of the Peninsular War that refers specifically to the conduct of the Guards, but there were many other occasions when they distinguished themselves in action. They honoured the traditions of the Household troops at Barrosa and Burgos, for example; and on 18th June 1815 when, as Wellington later said, the closing of the gates of Hougoumont decided the outcome of the battle of Waterloo – adding that 'no troops but the British could have held Hougoumont and only the best of them, at that.'

The officers of the Guards may have been mocked from time to time by the men of the Line regiments but when J.W. Fortescue, the great historian of the British Army, wrote that the officers of the Guards were able to command more respect from their men as a result of their upbringing, he was only echoing the thoughts of one of the Peninsular War's most lauded diarists. John Kincaid, of the 95th Rifles, regretted the fact that more aristocratic families of England did not send their sons into the Army, as they seemed to be able to command more willing obedience from their men, with less effort, than others. Fortescue went on to say that 'no one who knows anything of the subject will dispute the advantage which the habit of command, inherited through many generations and acquired in childhood, may confer upon a man.' This may well be reflected in the extremely low number of Court Martial cases involving the men of the Guards. In the archives of the Coldstream Guards, for instance, court martial records show that the vast majority of disciplinary cases involved only trifling offences, misdemeanours such as falling asleep on duty or getting drunk – the universal curse of the whole army. Indeed, on 4 March 1811 Wellington himself issued a General Order stating that since he took command of the army two years previous, there had yet to be a single soldier in the Brigade of Guards to

that the dinner there was cheaper and better than at the other clubs. It was an expensive business being an officer in the Guards; but in spite of this the clamour for commissions was often intense, and the rate of purchase the highest in the Army.

The socially élite Guards officers were often scorned and mocked by members of other regiments, and it would often delight the men of Line regiments to see Guards officers 'getting their hands dirty' as they struggled through the snow during the retreat to Corunna in 1809, or took part in the hectic forced march from Brussels to Quatre Bras in 1815. However, the Guards were among the best disciplined and most highly trained and effective of Wellington's (and Moore's) troops – witness the arrival of the 1st Foot Guards at Corunna after the harrowing retreat through the barren, snow-covered mountains of north-western Spain in January 1809. Moore's dishevel-

be brought before a general court martial, and not one of them had even been so much as confined in a public guard. This was praise indeed, and says much for the Guards' discipline and the men's respect for their officers.

As with all of Wellington's British troops the Guards were fiercely loyal to their regiments, a loyalty born out of comradeship and the sharing of the hardships of campaign life. But it was also a loyalty, of course, to king and country: the aristocratic classes from which the Guards drew their officers had much to lose should the spectre of republicanism materialise at home – in the shape either of Napoleon, or of home-grown anarchy and revolution. After all, revolution had only recently swept away the aristocracy in France, and with the beheading of Louis XVI, the ruling classes throughout the rest of Europe trembled lest the winds of violent change blow over their own lands. The legacies of the early Industrial Revolution in England may have begun to create an undercurrent of revolutionary fervour in Britain, stirred up by occasional radicals among displaced workers, the poor and the homeless, who looked to France for inspiration. Fortunately for Britain, there was an even stronger loyalty to king and country, and the great majority of Britons had no desire to see their homeland trodden underfoot by the Corsican upstart. Moreover, the broadsheets and satirists of the day did their job well, confronting a genuinely worried British public with savage cartoons illustrating the terrible consequences of a successful invasion by Napoleon. The French emperor was quickly transformed into the greatest bogeyman this nation had ever known, an ogre whose shadow loomed over the British Isles for almost 20 years.

Of course, the Guards officers were not exclusively aristocrats. They were also the sons of the landed gentry, often following their fathers and grandfathers into the same regiment – a tradition still maintained today. When they joined the Army they joined to see military service and to defend Britain's shores from the threat of Napoleon. But when they embarked upon service they did so not with any grimly militaristic outlook, but more often displaying the air of sportsmen off in search of honourable quarry and healthy exercise. We find amongst the Guards officers expert shots, keen hunters, trained judges of horses and greyhounds, naturalists, bota-

Major Sir John Guise, 3rd Foot Guards. He wears his full dress uniform with scarlet collar, edged gold.

nists and, of course, men with a great sense of style and fun.

Among many letters and memoirs recording the light-hearted determination of these young men to enjoy campaign life, we read of lavish dinner parties, served from silver; of luxuries and comforts of every kind, shipped out from home at the express order of gentlemen of the Guards; of fox hunting and wildfowling, race meetings and extravagant wagers. We read, particularly, of the army's constant struggle to limit their train of baggage animals on the march. Yet despite their pampered airs, the 'Gentlemen's sons' enjoyed no immunity from the dangers of battle, where they were expected to give an example of absolute unconcern for their own safety – and did so. Nor did their field beds and silver cutlery do much to ease the weariness of marching back and forth across the Iberian Peninsula, for a total which has been calculated at 6,000 miles. Apart from the occasional sad example like Sir Thomas Styles of the 1st Foot

An officer of the Coldstream Guards, c.1812. Although not wearing the uniform of a flank company, he is wearing a serpent and lion-mask waist belt clasp, which was usually worn by them.

The Light Company of the Coldstream Guards outside the château of Hougoumont during the Battle of Waterloo, 18 June 1815. They are wearing their white summer trousers and have oilskin covers over their shakos, with black tape chinstraps. The guardsman loading his musket, right centre, appears to have a huge haversack over his shoulder. After a painting by Dighton.

Guards, who cut his own throat soon after a punishing march to join his battalion, most of these young men put up with hardship and danger cheerfully.

John Mills is perhaps a typical example. Commissioned in the Coldstream Guards on 21 December 1809 at the age of 20, Mills joined the 1st Battalion Coldstream Guards in Portugal in December the following year. He was no son of the aristocracy, but had sufficient income to live rather well, to entertain, and to maintain a 'stud' consisting of a horse called Docktail (who was taken from the French at Salamonde) as well as two mare mules, Bess and Jenny, and a small mule called Turpin. Mills also supported his private servant, William, a soldier servant named Duckworth who looked after the animals, and Joseph, a Portuguese boy who helped him. He later increased his 'establishment' by employing a batman called Moore. From this modest example one can

only shudder to think of the amount of baggage that followed Wellington's army.

John Mills was, of course, first and foremost an officer in the Coldstream Guards but a cursory glance at his letters and diaries also reveals him to be a sportsman, never one to pass up the opportunity of a hunt, of shooting game, or of indulging in horseracing, coursing or playing cricket. He held card schools and dinner parties, and dined at monasteries and in the best hotels when in Lisbon. Wherever he went he noted the architecture and the agriculture, visited vineyards and sampled the local wines, and would make notes and sketches of wildlife (birds in particular). One is struck by the level of knowledge and attention to detail displayed in his letters and diaries, but he is typical of the young Guards officer on campaign. After the close of the Napoleonic Wars Mills became a 'man about town' amongst other things, and took up the mantle of Beau Brummel

following his demise. A great horse lover, he won many Gold Cups at Goodwood, became a member of the Royal Yacht Club, and later married a 'pretty heiress in London.'

The Honourable John Edward Cornwallis Rous, the son of the 1st Earl of Stradbroke, was a contemporary of Mills. Rous joined the 1st Battalion Coldstream Guards just before the battle of Salamanca in 1812 and, like Mills, he wrote an account of his experiences during the war. Rous took the danger and hardship of war in his stride, and his letters show that towards the end of hostilities he was more concerned at missing out on balls, and going to the opera in Bordeaux and Toulouse, than he was about staying alive on the battlefield. He bemoaned the fact that he missed the major race meetings back home, such as the Derby, as he was a great horse lover and maintained a sizeable stud in England. His letters are also full of the trials of maintaining a good table,

under difficult conditions, of his sporting exploits and his billets and bivouacs. He also displays a remarkable knowledge and assessment of the events, both political and military, elsewhere in Europe. Rous took his younger brother William to the Peninsula with him, in the hope of getting him an ensigncy in the Coldstream. William travelled with John throughout the campaign of 1812 before obtaining his commission in the regiment in December of that year. Rous later became the 2nd Earl of Stradbroke, and lived to the ripe age of 91, often recounting to his grandchildren his adventures in the Peninsula.

Both Mills and Rous are typical of the young Guards ensigns who fought in the Peninsula and at Waterloo. One could go into great detail describing the backgrounds and subsequent careers of dozens of Guards officers; but the few mentioned will give a sufficient flavour of the type that earned the Guards their reputation.

It is well known that Wellington loved to surround himself with 'bright young things', officers full of life who seemed to spark the same enthusiasm in him. The Brigades of Guards were usually kept close to his headquarters in the Peninsula; Wellington could often be found joking with their officers, and they were frequently invited to dinner with him. Raised to social ease, his young officers were equally comfortable in the dining room, on the dance floor and on the battlefield; and whenever Wellington chose to hold a ball they were very much in attendance and very much at home. One has only to look at the youthful, boyish faces of some of the Guards officers pictured elsewhere in this book to get an idea of the sort of character to be found at army headquarters,

Another version of the repulse of the Imperial Guard at Waterloo by the 1st Foot Guards. One slight error shows the battle honours just visible on the colour, left: 'Barrosa' and 'Corunna' should in fact be transposed.

Captain Francis Wheler Hood, 3rd Foot Guards, who was killed at the combat at Aire on 2 March 1814; from a painting by Raeburn. He is resting on his 1796-pattern infantry officer's sword.

many of whom maintained contact with their old commander after the wars. One young officer of the sort with which Wellington would surround himself was Lord James Hay of the 1st Foot Guards, who was presented to the Prince Regent at a ball just prior to leaving for the Waterloo campaign. The Prince was moved to say that he had never seen so handsome a young soldier in the uniform of the Guards. Unfortunately, Hay was later killed at Quatre Bras.

The senior ranks who led these young blades in battle were men who led from the front and served similar ideals and principles to their younger colleagues. Commanding the Guards at Hougoumont on 18 June 1815 was Lieutenant-Colonel James Macdonell, later to be called the bravest man at Waterloo. Macdonell, the third son of Duncan Macdonell of Glengarry, had served with distinction in the Peninsula. When the French gained entry into

Hougoumont it was Macdonell who was instrumental in closing the gates, and was seen walking around the courtyard carrying a huge log in his arms to help barricade the gates. Alexander Lord Saltoun, a lieutenant-colonel in the 1st Foot Guards, was also at Waterloo; the 15th Lord Saltoun commanded the Light Companies of the 1st Brigade of Guards, and had four horses shot beneath him. He also played a prominent part in the Guards' defeat of the Imperial Guard at the climax of the battle.

One last, humorous word on the officers of the Guards concerns one of the genuine aristocrats, Lord Alvanley, whose brothel account is preserved amongst the records of the Coldstream Guards. Apparently, Alvanley was due to depart for Spain in December 1808 when a certain Mr Derville, anxious that the outstanding debt should be paid lest Alvanley come to a sticky end, wrote asking for settlement.

The account makes intriguing reading, and includes such entries as 'one night with Mrs Dubois (grande blonde) £5 5s', 'an American lady, £10', and 'All night with Miss N. from the Boarding School, Chelsea, £5 5s'. His Lordship was an active fellow as his visits were made at times including Sunday mornings and five o'clock in the afternoon.

Rank and file

These were the officers; but what of the men? They were just as loyal to their country and to their regiment, but of course came from vastly different backgrounds. As with all private soldiers who joined the British Army they did so for various reasons ranging from boredom, and the lure of relatively regular pay and food, to a genuine thirst for adventure and, of course, escape from the law, women, debts or cruel masters. The difference in background and motive between those who were

Alexander, Lord Saltoun, in the uniform of a lieutenant, Light Company, 1st Foot Guards, c.1810. Saltoun initially commanded the Light Companies of the Guards at Hougoumont and later played a prominent part in the defeat of the Imperial Guard. With only six of the regulation ten buttons visible on his jacket, he was probably not a tall man, perhaps managing to fit only eight buttons onto it in all.

recruited into the ranks of the Foot Guards and those who joined ordinary Line regiments is insignificant; and it was presumably the training the former received which made the vital difference once they had donned the red jacket.

As already stated, the NCOs of the Guards were rated by Wellington as the best in the Army, and they simply would not tolerate any slovenliness either in appearance or in standards of discipline, as reflected in the above-mentioned court martial records. Of course, one can find instances of drunkenness among the regimental archives of the Guards. However it appears that the majority of these were offences committed at home and not while on campaign, when lives depended upon strict obedience to their officers' and NCOs' commands.

It might be useful to look at the backgrounds of two privates, who have since become rather celebrated in the history of the Foot Guards. Joseph Alston was one of the men who helped close the gates at Hougoumont during the Battle of Waterloo and is featured in the famous painting of the event by Robert Gibb. Alston enlisted in the 3rd Foot Guards at Birmingham on 12 September 1808 at the age of eighteen. Born at King's Norton near Worcester, he was a scribe by profession, was 5 feet 8 inches tall and had dark brown hair, a fair complexion and hazel eyes. Alston was therefore literate; and had a good character, as proved by his conduct at Waterloo, by which time he was a sergeant. He served for a further 18 years before being discharged on 8 August 1833.

Perhaps the most famous private of the Guards was Matthew Clay, who left one of the most detailed accounts of any private soldier at Waterloo. Clay enlisted in the 3rd Foot Guards in London just 18 months before Waterloo, on 6 December 1813 also at the age of eighteen. He was born at Blidworth near Nottingham, and by trade was a knitter or farm worker. He was 5 feet 7 inches tall, had a fresh complexion, grey eyes and fair hair, and is said to have had a very good character. Like Alston, Clay was discharged in 1833 having had a distinguished career in the Foot Guards.

Both men appear to have been of average height for the Foot Guards. When the 1st Battalion 1st Foot Guards was inspected in May 1809, after being brought up to strength following its ordeal during the retreat to Corunna, it was found that of the 1,203 men the average height of the Grenadier Company was 5 feet 11 inches, that of the Light Company 5 feet 8 inches, and that of the Battalion Companies 5 feet 7 inches.

SERVICE RECORD

On 1 August 1808 a force of around 9,500 British troops landed on the Portuguese coast north of Lisbon under the command of Sir Arthur Wellesley. It was the first step in Britain's involvement in the Peninsular War, which would see her army march back and forth across the Iberian Peninsula for six years before finally crossing the Pyrenees into France to help bring about the first downfall of Napoleon in 1814.

The Foot Guards' involvement in the Peninsular

War began in September 1808 when nearly 2,500 men of the 1st and 3rd Battalions 1st Foot Guards embarked at Ramsgate for the Peninsula, disembarking at Corunna at the end of October. The British Army in the Peninsula at this time was commanded by Sir John Moore, Wellesley having been recalled to England to face a court of enquiry following the Convention of Cintra. (This notorious agreement, reached by Wellesley's superior, had allowed the French whom he had defeated at Vimeiro to sail back to France in British ships with their accumulated plunder.) Unfortunately, by the time the Guards arrived in the Peninsula events had taken quite a different turn. Napoleon had come south in person to drive the British into the sea, and the 1st Foot Guards, forming part of the force under Sir David Baird, had hardly joined the main British army when Moore began his retreat to Corunna. The retreat began on Christmas Eve 1808 and finally ended with the Battle of Corunna on 16 January 1809. During this forced winter march over punishing terrain, all but a few of the better units lost discipline, and drunkenness and plundering were rife. The two battalions of the 1st Foot Guards, as we have seen, maintained their standards throughout the retreat.

The 1st Foot Guards were not to return to the Peninsula until the spring of 1810, but in the meantime the 1st Battalions of the Coldstream and 3rd Foot Guards were despatched, arriving in March and April 1809. In May of that year both battalions took part in the crossing of the river Douro which ended with the expulsion from Portugal of Marshal Soult. Just over two months later the Coldstream and 3rd Foot Guards were heavily involved at the Battle of Talavera, on 27–28 July. On the 28th the Guards' enthusiasm got the better of their discipline when they charged too far after the defeated French divisions of Lapisse and Sebastiani. Losses on this occasion were heavy, some 620 killed and wounded; but they re-formed and took their place in the line once again to help win the day for Wellesley – henceforward, Viscount Wellington.

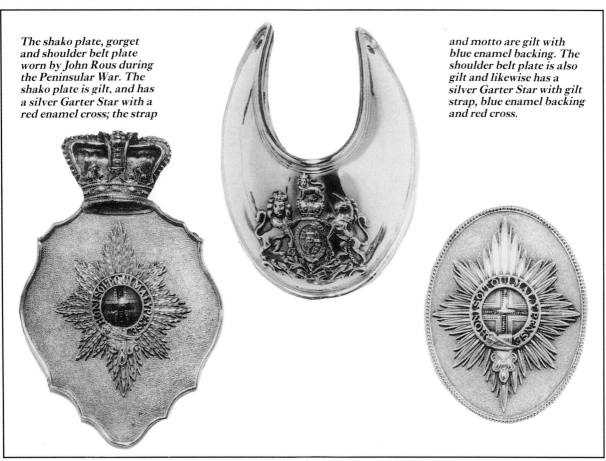

The shako plate, gorget and shoulder belt plate worn by John Rous during the Peninsular War. The shako plate is gilt, and has a silver Garter Star with a red enamel cross; the strap and motto are gilt with blue enamel backing. The shoulder belt plate is also gilt and likewise has a silver Garter Star with gilt strap, blue enamel backing and red cross.

It was to be a year before Wellington's army fought another major battle. This took place at Busaco, but although the two battalions of Foot Guards were present they were not directly involved in the day's fighting. Following the battle Wellington retreated into the Lines of Torres Vedras, and it was not until March 1811 that he emerged in pursuit of Massena's starving, retreating army.

Meanwhile in the south at Cadiz, which was under siege from the French, a British force of around 4,000 men under Sir Thomas Graham sailed along the coast to Tarifa before marching back upon

the rear of the French, assisted by 10,000 Spaniards under General La Pena. On 5 March 1811 the allies clashed with the French at Barrosa. During this engagement the Brigade of Guards under General Dilkes – consisting of six companies of the 1st Foot Guards, two companies of the Coldstream and three companies of the 3rd Foot Guards – distinguished itself in fierce fighting atop the hill of Barrosa.

The main body of Wellington's army next took the field at Fuentes de Oñoro on 3–5 May 1811. Outnumbered by almost 10,000 men, Wellington won a hard-earned victory during which the Coldstream and 3rd Foot Guards played their part, sustaining 135 casualties.

By the end of the year Wellington was in a position to begin his drive into Spain, however he first had to take the two frontier fortresses of Ciudad Rodrigo and Badajoz. At Ciudad Rodrigo, in January 1812, the Coldstream and 3rd Foot Guards took their turn in the trenches, digging and constructing batteries. The actual assault was delivered by the 3rd and Light Divisions; but the two battalions had played their part, and Ciudad Rodrigo was later awarded to them as a battle honour. The Foot Guards next saw

Left: Sergeant and private, 1st Foot Guards, 1812. Both men are wearing their greatcoats, and have covered their shakos and plumes with their foul-weather oilskin covers. From 1808 sergeants were ordered to wear the facing colour of their regiment, dark blue in this case, on their collar and cuffs. The sergeant carries his nine foot-long spontoon. An aquatint by I.C. Stadler after a drawing by Charles Hamilton Smith.

Right: Two privates of a Battalion Company, 1st Foot Guards, 1812. Both men wear their grey trousers tucked into their gaiters, the style worn at Waterloo; usually the trousers were worn outside. The plume is white over red, worn with white worsted cotton chain and tassels. The shako plate is brass and has an embossed Garter Star with a reversed GR in the centre of it. Aquatint by I.C. Stadler after a drawing by Charles Hamilton Smith.

service as part of the covering force under Sir Thomas Graham during the siege operations at Badajoz, ensuring that there was no interference from the French, under Marshal Soult, who were approaching from the south.

Badajoz fell to Wellington on 6 April, and with both fortresses in his hands he began to advance deeper into Spain. On 22 July 1812 he inflicted a crushing defeat on the French under Marmont at Salamanca, the French suffering some 15,000 casualties including 7,000 prisoners. Only the Light Companies of the Coldstream and 3rd Foot Guards were involved in the battle, being detailed to hold the vital position of the village of Los Arapiles. From Salamanca the road turned south-east towards Madrid; and after a short spell there Wellington moved

north-west to lay siege to Burgos. On this occasion he was to be unsuccessful: it was perhaps the most depressing operation of the war for him, as a series of assaults were repulsed by a tenacious garrison. The Guards performed well during the siege operations, earning praise in Wellington's dispatches; he added sourly that it was a pity the rest of the army had not performed likewise. The operations dragged on from September to October 1812 before Wellington was finally forced to abandon the attempt, and with large French numbers gathering close by the army was compelled to withdraw first towards Salamanca and then all the way to the Portuguese border. This was a painful experience somewhat reminiscent of the retreat to Corunna.

During the retreat the Coldstream and 3rd Foot

Guards had been joined by the 1st and 3rd Battalions of the 1st Foot Guards, these latter being brigaded together to form the 1st Guards Brigade while the 1st Battalions of the Coldstream and 3rd Foot Guards formed the 2nd Brigade of Guards. In November 1812, 800 men of the 1st Foot Guards, and 400 each from the Coldstream and the 3rd Foot Guards, were sent from England to Holland to take part in the attack on Bergen-op-Zoom, an expedition commanded by Sir Thomas Graham. This campaign lasted until March the following year when, after an abortive assault on the place, an armistice was agreed.

By the spring of 1813 Wellington's army was strong enough to repeat the thrust into Spain; and in May of that year his army advanced across the Tras-o-Montes towards Vittoria. It was there that he smashed the French army under Joseph Bonaparte on 21 June – only prevented from inflicting even more damage when his men stopped to plunder the enormous wealth of Joseph's baggage train. After Vittoria Wellington headed towards the Pyrenees, and by the end of September he had fought his way over them and was ready to cross into southern France. While Wellington had been busy in the mountains the Guards had been involved in the siege of the coastal stronghold of San Sebastian, which fell on 31 August 1813. The two Brigades of Guards suffered 127 casualties during the assault. With San Sebastian in his hands there was nothing standing between Wellington and France and, on 7 October 1813, the operations that would see his army enter Napoleon's heartland began with the crossing of the river Bidassoa, during which the Guards spearheaded the left wing of the army. There was more hard fighting to be done as the Brigades of Guards took part in the crossing of the rivers Nivelle and Adour. During the latter operation, on 23 February 1814, the 2nd Brigade of Guards made a bold crossing in small boats covered by some Riflemen and a couple of salvoes of Congreve rockets. After the crossing of the Adour the main part of Wellington's army pressed on towards Toulouse while the Guards remained behind to lay siege to Bayonne.

On 12 April the Peninsular War finally came to an end following the Battle of Toulouse, although – as Napoleon had actually abdicated on 4 April – the battle was an unnecessary one. However, for the Guards there was still one more major action. On 14 April,

Ensign William Pitt, Coldstream Guards, killed during the sortie from Bayonne. The gilt gorget has blue rosettes and the gilt shoulder belt plate has a silver Garter Star, blue enamel strap backing, and white centre with red enamel cross. Miniature by Thomas Heaphy. This is probably a very accurate picture, as Heaphy travelled to the Peninsula in 1812 to paint portraits of various British officers.

whether out of ignorance or malice, the governor of Bayonne, Thouvenot, decided to launch a sortie during which the two Brigades of Guards suffered some 508 men killed, wounded or taken prisoner in a bloody and totally futile action. With the war finally at an end the troops began to return home; the 1st Brigade of Guards sailed from France on 26–27 July 1814, the 2nd Brigade following soon afterwards.

On 26 February 1815 Napoleon, after just ten months of exile on the island of Elba, began his last desperate gamble for power. Once again the Allied armies of Europe began to muster their forces, and two brigades of Guards were formed as part of Wellington's army. The 1st Brigade consisted of the 2nd and 3rd Battalions 1st Foot Guards under Peregrine Maitland; the 2nd Brigade, under Sir John Byng, consisted of the 2nd Battalions of the

Coldstream and 3rd Foot Guards. Together the two brigades formed the 1st Division of the army.

Napoleon opened the 1815 campaign by striking at the armies of Wellington and Blücher, whose Prussian army was formed on Wellington's left flank. Basically his plan was to defeat Blücher first, while Ney held Wellington in check, after which both would turn against Wellington, defeat his isolated army and take Brussels. In theory this would bring about an early end to the war. Napoleon duly mauled Blücher at Ligny on 16 June while Ney and Wellington fought a bloody and inconclusive action at Quatre Bras. However, instead of withdrawing away from Wellington, Blücher retreated due north, parallel withUWellington's own retreating army, so that they were able to converge on 18 June on the position at Mont St Jean to fight the momentous Battle of Waterloo. During the battle the Light Companies of the Guards held the vital post of the château of Hougoumont on Wellington's right flank. Originally intended to be nothing more than a diversion, it soon became the scene of a battle within a battle as whole divisions of French were poured into the fight. Eventually all but two companies of the Coldstream Guards were fed into the château, along with the remaining companies of the 3rd Foot Guards, the two battalions of the 1st Foot Guards remaining in the line on the main position on the ridge behind Hougoumont. In spite of repeated heavy attacks from French infantry and artillery, which set the buildings alight, Hougoumont remained in British hands throughout the entire day.

The two battalions of the 1st Foot Guards had

'Now Maitland, now's your time!' calls Wellington as the 1st Foot Guards hurl back the Imperial Guard at Waterloo. The Grenadiers, bottom left, never wore their bearskins in battle, in spite of popular belief, saving them only for State occasions or parades.

Right: Officers' gilt shoulder belt plate, 1st Foot Guards, 1815.

recognition of their part played in defeating the Imperial Guard the Prince Regent bestowed upon the 1st Foot Guards the title of 'Grenadier', the full name of the regiment becoming the First or Grenadier Regiment of Foot Guards.

UNIFORMS

The section on campaign dress deals with non-regulation items of clothing and with the effects that campaign life had on the uniforms; initially we cover the regulation uniform.

Officers

The officers of the Foot Guards wore three uniforms: full dress; undress; and service dress. Full dress was worn at Court, at royal parades and at balls, which in the case of the Guards was fairly often. The long-tailed coat was scarlet, with a scarlet collar laced gold all round, and blue lapels that were 5 inches across at the top, tapering to 3 inches at the bottom. Gold lace loops were spaced according to the regiment: singly for the 1st Foot Guards; in pairs for the Coldstream; and in threes for the 3rd Foot Guards. The cuffs were blue, round, and had two bands of

meanwhile spent the day under fire along with the rest of the Allied army on the ridge. However, when Napoleon decided to commit his Imperial Guard to the attack at the crucial moment of the battle, the 1st Foot Guards found that they were about to bear the main brunt of the attack. A column of the Imperial Guard duly reached the crest of the Allied position, but at the vital moment Wellington, who had come forward to direct the Guards himself, ordered them to stand up, make ready and fire. Maitland's Guards seemed to appear from nowhere and delivered a series of devastating volleys into the shocked ranks of Frenchmen, who were driven back in disorder. The final blow had been delivered by Wellington's Foot Guards; and with Blücher's Prussians joining the fight in ever increasing numbers the battle was won. As

gold lace around the upper edge, the lower band being wider than the upper. On the cuffs and under each pocket flap there were three buttons for the 1st and 3rd Foot Guards and four buttons for the Coldstream. The coat was long-skirted, with horizontal pocket flaps which were laced all round. The pocket flaps were edged in broad gold lace, two bands of which ran down the edges of the folds in the back to form two diamond shapes around the hip buttons. The turnbacks were of white kerseymere and were gold-laced and edged in blue, with embroidered skirt ornaments, the respective regimental star being set in a half-wreath of laurel on blue cloth. A coat of this sort can be seen in the National Army Museum, London; it was worn by Lieutenant-Colonel William Miller, 1st Foot Guards, who was mortally wounded at Quatre Bras.

Undress uniform was a plain scarlet coat with blue lapels, collar and cuffs, the collar and lapels laced all round in gold; the cuffs were round and also edged with gold lace. As on all Guards officers' coats the buttons were at regimental spacing on the lapels: ten equally spaced for the 1st Foot Guards, ten in pairs for the Coldstream, and nine in threes for the 3rd Foot Guards. (However, evidence has shown that it must have been difficult to fit all of these buttons on the coat of an officer of small stature.) The skirts of the coat had laced diamond decorations at the hips and vertical bars down the seams to the bottoms of the skirts. The pockets were laced gold all round, and the turnbacks were of white kerseymere edged gold decorated at the junction with sycamore seed-shaped blue patches upon which were embroidered sprays of palm leaves. The officers of the Light Companies often wore the undress jacket for full dress although the dress regulations of 1802 state that a long-tailed full dress coat was to be worn by light infantry company officers for full dress.

The third uniform was the service dress worn on campaign. This was in effect a version of the undress coat. Until 1812 only Light Company officers wore short-skirted jackets. After this date short skirts were introduced for all officers, an order which, judging from the reaction of John Mills of the Coldstream, was met with some apprehension: 'We are all in consternation at the idea of the dress of the army being altered from cocked hats and coats to caps and jackets. Ye heavens, what will become of crooked legs, large heads, and still larger hinder parts?' The service jacket was scarlet with blue lapels, collar and cuffs, all edged with gold lace. The buttons were of regimental spacing. Officers of Battalion Companies wore the regimental stars as skirt ornaments, while Light Company officers had bugle horns (the latter often wore their service jackets instead of their undress uniform).

Officers' waistcoats were single-breasted and of white face cloth; they had high collars and short skirts, two pockets with outside flaps and three or

An unusual variation of officers' headdress worn during the Peninsular War. The shako is made of strong black felt, with a black ribbed silk band around the bottom, black silk cockade, silver half-ball button and green cords. It also has an oilskin lining. The feather is not original. The inside of the shako is stamped with the inscription, 'Hat for (?). Paid; two shillings (value 12/-). Makers C. Oliphant, Cockspur Street, London.'

four buttons at the hip. As on all Guards jackets the buttons, of small size on the waistcoats, were in regimental spacing, but there was no lace or embroidery around the buttonholes.

Epaulettes had gold-laced straps about 5 inches long and $2\frac{1}{2}$ inches wide; there were two rows of bright gold bullions, the outer row being 3 inches deep. Ensigns wore only one right-hand epaulette with the appropriate embroidered device; captains wore two, also with embroidered devices, and field officers similar. Captains of Grenadier Companies wore epaulettes with silver grenades, captains of Light Companies silver bugle horns; these officers wore their epaulettes over their flank company wings. Ensigns and lieutenants of flank companies wore their wings only, with either grenades or bugle horns. The officer's sash was made of crimson silk and was 6 inches wide and some 7 feet 4 inches long, with a 10 inch tassel fringe. In the Light Company the sash had silk crimson cords and bell rope tassels.

On campaign grey-blue trousers were worn, usually over half boots with a grey strap under the instep. Many officers also took to wearing blue-grey riding overalls, reinforced around the bottoms with

Lieutenant-Colonel Sir Henry Sullivan, Bt., Coldstream Guards. Sullivan was another casualty of the sortie from Bayonne. His shako bears the gold banding around the false front which was usually removed during active service and replaced with the normal black tape. There is little evidence to show that the 1812-pattern shako was ever worn in the Peninsula except by drafts sent out very late in the war. Sullivan, however, almost certainly did wear one, having only returned to the Peninsula in March 1814. After a painting by Edridge.

Lieutenant-Colonel George Collier, Coldstream Guards, painted wearing the uniform of a flank company. Collier was killed during the sortie from Bayonne in 1814.

leather cuffs. White kerseymere breeches were also worn. At Court, or on full dress parade, white silk stockings were worn with shoes. Also worn at Court were white linen gaiters with black buttons and a buckled strap, 4 inches above the knee. A variety of boots were worn including Hessians, Hussar boots, top boots or half boots. More information on foot-wear is contained in the section on campaign dress.

Other Ranks

In the Foot Guards the sergeants' jackets were unusual in that they had gold lace. The jacket was scarlet and lined throughout – the sleeve with linen and the other parts with white serge. The jacket had short skirts which were sewn back, lined with white serge and edged with gold lace. It was a single-breasted jacket, buttoned across the front, and the left side was edged with gold. The buttons were gilt and regimentally spaced; the loops were of gold lace – eight or nine evenly spaced bastion-shaped loops for the 1st Foot Guards, ten pointed-shaped loops in pairs for the Coldstream, and nine pointed-shaped loops in groups of three for the 3rd Foot Guards. The collar, cuffs, wings and shoulder straps were dark blue and trimmed with gold lace. The cuffs were edged with gold lace with three buttons and loops for the 1st and 3rd Foot Guards, and four buttons and loops in pairs for the Coldstream. The gold lace loops were the same pattern as those on the front of the jacket. The pockets on the skirts were figured all round with gold lace and had buttons and loops: four for the 1st Foot Guards; four in two pairs for the Coldstream; and three for the 3rd Foot Guards. The rear of the jacket was decorated with a diamond of gold lace between the hip buttons and another diamond under each hip button. A bar of gold lace ran down the seam to the bottom edge. The shoulder wings of the Grenadier and Light Companies were dark blue, decorated with six darts of gold lace in the regimental pattern and trimmed with a gold fringe.

The jackets of corporals and privates were similar to those of sergeants except that they were of red cloth, had white worsted lace instead of gold, and had woollen tufts on the shoulder straps and white edging on the wings. NCOs' and privates' waistcoats were white, with a standing collar, round cuffs and shoulder straps all in dark blue. The waistcoat doubled as a fatigue jacket and was worn for drills and often when out foraging. On State occasions NCOs and privates of the Foot Guards wore white cloth breeches and long gaiters, the latter extended well over the knee, and were fastened by black buttons. For full dress they wore black woollen gaiters which were fastened by ten small white metal buttons. On campaign short grey gaiters were worn, strapped under the instep, beneath grey or grey-blue trousers or overalls. In summer white trousers were also worn. A Dighton print of the Coldstream Guards at Hougoumont shows them wearing white trousers, as does a Lawson print of the 3rd Foot Guards at Talavera. A De Loutherbourg painting of the 1st Foot Guards departing for the Peninsula at Ramsgate in 1808 shows the men wearing a variety of legwear including white trousers buttoned at the sides, blue-grey trousers, and white breeches with black gaiters.

Headdress

For full dress, undress and service dress Guards

officers still wore the bicorne or cocked hat. Worn 'fore and aft' the hat was made from felt with gold edging and tassels, although on active service the edging was of black tape. Plumes were of cut feathers, coloured as for infantry shakos, and were secured behind a small black cockade with a gold lace loop running down from it. However, in 1812 officers of all regiments of the Army were expected to wear the 'stove-pipe' shako, already worn by other ranks and Light Infantry officers. Introduced in 1806, the shako was cylindrical in shape and made of strong felt. The shako plate was brass and bore the Royal Cypher within the garter, the Crown above, the Royal Lion below and trophies on either side. On the shako plate of the Light Companies of the Guards the Royal Lion was replaced by a bugle horn. Officers wore cut feather plumes on their shakos whilst other ranks wore woollen tufts. The colours of the plumes were the same as in the Line regiments: white over red for Battalion Companies, green for the Light Company, and white for the Grenadier Company.

Another change of headdress came about in 1812 with the introduction of the 'Waterloo' or 'Belgic' shako. This was made of strong felt for other ranks, coarse beaver for sergeants and fine beaver – with a taller false front to give the impression of height – for officers. A festoon of white worsted chain and tassels was fixed across the front for other ranks, of

Two views of a private of the 3rd Foot Guards, c.1807, after watercolours by Atkinson. These show the uniform of the 3rd Foot Guards just prior to the Peninsular War. He wears tight overalls buttoned all the way up the side. He also wears his hair tied back in a 'queue', one of the much hated practices abolished in 1808. He has no knapsack but carries a rolled blanket. Note the regimental star on his cartridge box.

The 1812-pattern 'Belgic' shako. These examples belonged to a line infantry regiment, the Guards having their own shako plate. Note also the bugle horn fixed to the side of the shako, signifying a light company. Compare this with the photograph on the right, showing the manner in which the Guards' Light Infantry wore theirs.

gold cord for sergeants and of mixed gold and crimson chain cord and tassels for officers. The Light Companies wore green worsted chain and tassels. The plume was fitted to the left side by a small button within a black cockade. Whereas the shako plate for the Line regiments was of a universal design the Foot Guards wore brass plates adorned with their own regimental badge. Officers' shako plates were gilt and had enamelled centres. Although the 'Waterloo' shako saw service during the Waterloo campaign, there is little evidence to suggest that it was worn by rank and file in the Peninsula, other than by drafts that came out late in the war. Officers, however, may have worn it. Portraits, such as that of Lieutenant-Colonel Sir Henry Sullivan of the Coldstream, survive showing them with the shako. Many officers wrote home asking for the new pattern to be sent out to them. Some, like Ensign John Rous of the Coldstream, wrote asking for the new cap with gold edging around the false front; although this version of the cap may have been worn, it was the norm to remove the gold banding when on active service. All shakos, and for that matter all cocked hats whilst on service, could be protected with an oilskin cover in wet weather. Officers of the Guards retained their cocked hats for full dress parades, State duties, balls and for undress.

In the Grenadier Companies bearskins were worn on full dress parades only. Made of black bearskin, they were 16 inches tall and had a brass or gilt plate on the front bearing the full Royal Arms. By the time of the Waterloo campaign a small black leather peak had been added to the front. The white plume, 12 inches high, was worn on the left side of the bearskin secured in a socket. Officers' and NCOs' bearskins had gold chains and tassels, privates having white worsted cotton cords and tassels.

It will be of interest to note some of the prices given for these items of equipment, as recorded in the archives of the Coldstream Guards. For example, 24

December 1810, amongst a shipment of clothing and equipment sent out to the Peninsula to replace items lost during 1809, we find the following:

3 regimental caps @ 7s each	£ 1	1s	
3 feathers @ 9d each		2s	3d
1 regimental coat @ 19s 6d each		19s	6d
33 waistcoats @ 5s 6d each	£ 9	1s	6d
52 pairs of breeches @ 7s 10d each	£20	7s	4d
97 pairs of gaiters @ 4s each	£19	8s	
Total	£50	19s	7d

A year later, in November 1811, the headquarters of the Coldstream Guards in London received a request for the following items of which the 1st Battalion, then in Portugal, were said to be in dire need: 1 sergeant major's frock; 13 sergeants' jackets; 24 privates' jackets; 73 sergeants' sashes; 1,270 shirts; 1,000 pairs of soles and heels; 500 turnkeys, prickers, worms and brushes; and 400 black stocks.

The reference to the 1,000 pairs of soles and heels is interesting. One can only assume that the army would rather keep the regimental cobblers busy than issue new boots altogether. (For more details of the Guards boots see the section on campaign dress.) One should also note the reference to the 500 prickers and turnkeys. Attention is often drawn to instances of ramrods being fired away in haste by panicking infantrymen; however, without prickers and turnkeys muskets could also be rendered useless by fouling barrels and firing pans. It was important, therefore, that the men be issued with these small but vital pieces of equipment whenever replacements were needed.

Rank Distinctions

Officers

During the Peninsular and Waterloo campaigns the officers of the Foot Guards wore the following rank distinctions. It should be noted that Captains of Grenadier or Light Companies wore their epaulettes over the wings.

Colonels, Lieutenant-Colonels and Majors of Battalion Companies: Two epaulettes with bullions, with Royal Crowns and the regimental star on the straps of both.
Captains of Battalion Companies: Two epaulettes with bullions with only the regimental star on the strap.

The false front of a light infantry company shako, Coldstream Guards, with the bugle horn badge above the brass shako plate. The shako was once part of the collection of

Sergeant Major Cotton, and was presumably picked up off the battlefield of Waterloo. The collection was auctioned off at the turn of the century.

Captains commanding Grenadier or Light Infantry Companies: Two epaulettes with bullions worn over the wings and with either silver bugle horns or grenades worn above the regimental star.
Lieutenants and Ensigns of Battalion Companies: One epaulette with bullion worn on the right shoulder only with the regimental star on the shoulder strap.
Lieutenants and Ensigns of Grenadier or Light Infantry Companies: A wing on each shoulder decorated with either bugle horns or grenades.

NCOs

In 1802 a new system of rank distinctions for NCOs and corporals was introduced. Instead of the old shoulder knots and epaulettes, chevrons were introduced both for the Foot Guards and the Line Infantry. In the three regiments of Foot Guards the chevrons were worn as follows:
Sergeant Major: Four gold lace chevrons on dark blue cloth.
Colour Sergeant (from July 1813): Three gold lace chevrons on dark blue cloth, with a crimson King's

Colour placed upon the chevrons with the Royal Crown above and crossed swords below it.

Sergeant: Three gold lace chevrons on dark blue cloth.

Drum Major: Same as sergeants.

Corporals: Two white worsted lace chevrons on dark blue cloth.

Chosen Man (lance corporal): A single white worsted lace chevron on dark blue cloth.

Chevrons were worn on the right sleeve. There is little evidence to show that the sergeants of the Grenadier and Light Companies wore their chevrons on both arms, as was the practice in the Line infantry regiments. NCOs also wore their chevrons on the right sleeves of their greatcoats.

Another rank distinction was the sergeant's sash. These were initially crimson, with a white stripe in the 1st Foot Guards, plain crimson in the Coldstream, and crimson with a blue and white stripe in the 3rd Foot Guards. By the time of Waterloo, however, all sashes are presumed to have been plain crimson.

CAMPAIGN DRESS

Given the physical circumstances of campaign life, and the relatively relaxed attitude to 'uniformity' in battle, it was inevitable that some non-regulation and unusual items of dress came to be worn by officers and men even of the Foot Guards during the Peninsular and Waterloo campaigns. As the impracticality and deficiencies of some items of uniform became apparent, and as supplies of new clothing became erratic, a great deal of improvisation began to occur. Robert Mercer of the 3rd Foot Guards wrote on 22 December 1810 – still at an early stage of the Peninsular War – 'Every person here dresses as he likes. These fancy dresses occasion much surprise and horror to the martinets who arrive from London.' This improvisation was possible due to the large amount of clothing fashioned from locally purchased cloth, which was usually coloured brown. Scarlet and red jackets alike lost their colour in the heat, dust and rain. Jackets, of course, were usually protected by the wearing of greatcoats, but these were often so badly made that they fell apart after a short time; indeed, the archives of the Coldstream Guards record that when the regiment departed from Ciudad Rodrigo in 1812 the men simply left their coats in the breach or on the glacis.

Footwear was one of the great problems in Wellington's army. During the first campaign in the Peninsula, the ill-fated Corunna campaign, the boots issued to the army were exposed as being of wretched quality, cheap and totally inadequate, so much so that some soldiers said they broke up on the first day of the campaign. During the retreat of Moore's army through the mountains of Galicia the British Army endured terrible deprivations, made worse by the poor footwear issued to the men; boots and shoes were simply sucked off by the slush and mud, and hundreds of men were forced to march barefooted, leaving bloody trails in the snow as testament to their boots' inadequacies.

When the wreckage of Moore's army reached England there was one particularly interested spectator standing on the dock, watching in horror as the

Other ranks' shako plate, 1st Foot Guards, 1815. The plate is brass with an embossed Star of the Order of the Garter, with GR reversed in the centre.

dishevelled, ghost-like figures dragged themselves along the quayside, their lacerated and festering feet swathed in tattered bandages. The shocked onlooker was Marc Isambard Brunel, the father of the great engineer Isambard Kingdom Brunel. Marc Brunel was an inventor, and when he saw the miserable wretches coming off the ships he immediately began to enquire as to just how many men had been lost or had suffered due to poor footwear. The results of his enquiries came as something of a shock, figures revealing that as many men were lost through faulty footwear as from enemy action. Upon examining the boots Brunel found that between the thin inner and outer soles there was a layer of clay, needless to say, as soon as the boot was immersed in water this dissolved. Brunel set to work designing an improved boot for the Army, and the following year filed a patent for it. It was to be a further two years, however, before the British government decided to place an order for Brunel to supply all boots for the Army; but once this had been done production climbed to some 400 pairs per day. The issue of the new boots only began towards the close of the Peninsular War, by which time Wellington's men had resorted to several different alternatives to the standard issue footwear; but when Wellington's Foot Guards stood up to defeat the Imperial Guard at Waterloo they were wearing the Brunel boot.

In the meantime the problem was addressed in various ways by soldiers on campaign, ranging from the use of captured enemy footwear to the improvisation of moccasins, made from cow hide cut to the shape of the feet. On 28 March 1812 Ensign John Lucie Blackman of the Coldstream wrote from Abrantes: 'Our reason for staying here so long is that the men may get new shoes and other necessities they may be in want of as they will not have another opportunity till we arrive at Elvas.' These shoes must have been of poor quality; only four months later, following the battle of Salamanca, Blackman wrote that the Guards had 'marched their shoes off'. With no prospect of replacements, they adopted the mode of footwear used by the Spanish muleteers. The raw hide of a freshly killed ration bullock was laid flat and the man's foot placed on it; a sufficient piece of hide was then cut to cover the foot, and thonged together into a crude sandal or moccasin. This was most comfortable to wear, so much so that when the Guards entered Madrid many of them could not be persuaded to give them up for captured French shoes found in the Retiro. Many of the Guards still lacked shoes the following year when they began the Pyrenees campaign. Fortunately they were provided with the light hempen sandals made and worn by the local people, and these were well suited to the steep, slippery slopes of the mountains.

The flimsiness of contemporary boots can be illustrated by an anecdote from Ensign Rees Gronow of the 1st Foot Guards, who recalled that when a fellow officer, Sir John Shelley, went to see his

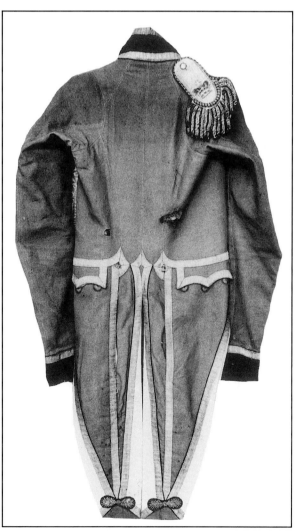

The coatee worn by Ensign Scott, 3rd Foot Guards, who was wounded at the Battle of Talavera; the bullet hole is easily visible beneath the right shoulder blade. The epaulette has obviously been added at a later date.

bootmaker, Hoby's of St James's, he complained that his boots had split in several places. Upon being asked how this had happened, Shelley replied, 'Why, in walking to my stable.' Hoby was taken aback by this: 'Walking to your stable! I made the boots for riding, not walking.' On another occasion Hoby was visited by Ensign Horace Churchill, also of the 1st Foot Guards, who said that his boots were so ill-made that he would never use Hoby again. The value of his previous custom had been such that when he left Hoby said to his assistant, 'John, close the shutters. It is all over with us. I must shut up shop; Ensign Churchill withdraws his custom from me.' Other evidence for the short life-span of English-made boots can be found in the letters from Guards officers.

Although officers and NCOs of the Foot Guards took great pride in their appearance, the rigours of the Peninsula campaign took their toll, and before long their uniforms were quite different from those worn in St James's Street and Pall Mall. Indeed, the overall appearance of the Guards was such that Ensign John Stepney Cowell of the Coldstream was moved to write in 1812 that 'in the haberdashery line we were all a little like those troops with which Falstaff, from a delicate sense of propriety, would not march through Coventry.' Changes to the regulation uniform were made purely out of necessity, and although the NCOs did their best to ensure the men looked their best, after a couple of Spanish summers and Portuguese winters even they were forced to accept the realities of

Other ranks' shako plate, 3rd Foot Guards, 1815. Brass, with an embossed Star of the Order of the Thistle with a thistle in the centre.

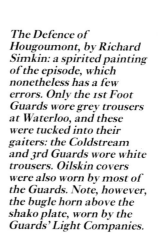

The Defence of Hougoumont, by Richard Simkin: a spirited painting of the episode, which nonetheless has a few errors. Only the 1st Foot Guards wore grey trousers at Waterloo, and these were tucked into their gaiters: the Coldstream and 3rd Guards wore white trousers. Oilskin covers were also worn by most of the Guards. Note, however, the bugle horn above the shako plate, worn by the Guards' Light Companies.

campaign life. Indeed, Wellington himself said he cared little what his men looked like; in one of the most quoted passages from Peninsular War literature, Lieutenant William Grattan of the 88th says that provided they came into the field well appointed and with sixty rounds of ammunition, the Commander-in-Chief 'never looked to see whether their trousers were black, blue or grey ... scarcely two officers were dressed alike.' But if Wellington cared little what his men looked like, at least the officers of the Guards tried to look their best, and many tailors were sent out to the Peninsula to ensure that at least some level of regularity prevailed. John Mills of the Coldstream relates that his battalion had taken on a French tailor captured from the enemy, who had all the latest Paris fashions!

During the cold winters in the Peninsula many of the Guards took to pulling down the sleeves of their long Welsh flannel shirts over their hands and tying them to form a sort of crude glove. The officers could

The Closing of the Gates at Hougoumont, by Robert Gibbs. An accurate painting of the episode, as Colonel Macdonnell and his men strain to close the gates in the face of a tremendous French surge. Once again, grey trousers are shown instead of white.

not do this, so a number of them had 'muffatees' sent out from England, which were normally knitted by 'the prettiest ladies we know', according to Ensign Rous. When he wrote home on 17 September 1813 to ask for some muffatees, he said that they were worn by a few officers; but that the ladies should not knit any for the soldiers, as it would make them too tender, adding that they would not keep them more than six hours! When he received the muffatees he wrote home, saying, 'You may depend on my taking the greatest possible care of the Muffatees, which will be of great use in the winter, at the same time you may be assured that the soldiers will never keep anything that they are not obliged, nor are they permitted on service to have anything in their possession which is not a regimental necessary. One would easily be lost, but to replace it would be difficult, and every soldier

has a long Welsh flannel waistcoat, with sleeves, and does not suffer at all from cold in the wrist.' Nevertheless, a great deal of non-regulation clothing was worn by both the officers and men, particularly following a battle or successful storming of a town, when captured French clothing and equipment would often be taken in large quantities. The extremes of the Iberian weather caused both officers and men to adopt suitable measures. Umbrellas, for instance, were very fashionable amongst the officers of the Guards, not only to keep themselves dry, as witnessed in the celebrated 'incident of the umbrellas' before Bayonne in December 1813, but also to provide shade from the blistering summer sun.

As the war proceeded and Wellington advanced into northern Spain, the army was supplied through the ports on the northern coast, rather than through Lisbon with its consequent long trek across hundreds of miles in order to reach the marching army. The army became better supplied, and clothing and equipment were issued more regularly.

One wonders what those Guards who had been at

1st Foot Guards embarking
for Corunna, 1808:
1: Private, 1st Battalion
2: Officer, 1st Battalion
3: Sergeant, 1st Battalion

A

1st Foot Guards retreating to Corunna, 1809:
1: Private, 1st Battalion
2: Sergeant, 1st Battalion
3: Officer, 1st Battalion

WRV. 93

B

Third Foot Guards, Talavera, 1809:
1: Sergeant
2: Officer
3: Corporal

C

Light Infantry Company Coldstream Guards, Salamanca, 1812:
1: Private   2: Officer   3: Sergeant

D

Foraging in the Peninsula:
1: Corporal, Coldstream Guards, undress
2: Officer, Coldstream Guards, undress
3: Private, Coldstream Guards, Light Infantry Company

WRJ. 93

E

Peninsula, 1812
1: The Honourable W. Dawson, 1st Foot Guards
2: Daniel Mackinnon, Coldstream Guards
3: The Honourable Orlando Bridgeman, 1st Foot Guards

F

The Pyrenees, 1813
1: Officer, 1st Foot Guards
2: Officer, Coldstream Guards
3: Officer, 3rd Foot Guards

G

Musicians, 3rd Foot Guards
1: Drum Major
2: Bugler
3: Drummer

H

1st Foot Guards, St James' Palace
1: Sergeant, Grenadier Company
2: Private, Grenadier Company
3: Officer, Grenadier Company

I

The Waterloo Ball, 15 June 1815
1: Officer, Battalion Company,
1st Foot Guards
2: Officer, Grenadier Company,
3rd Foot Guards

3: Officer, Light Infantry Company,
Coldstream Guards

J

Hougoumont, 18 June 1815
1: Officer, Coldstream Guards
2: Pioneer, Coldstream Guards
3: Private, Coldstream Guards

K

Waterloo, 1815
1: Colour Sergeant Charles Wood,
3rd Battalion, 1st Foot Guards

1

WRJ.93

L

Barrosa looked like by the end of the 1812 campaign. A brigade consisting of six companies of the 2nd Battalion 1st Foot Guards, and three companies each of the Coldstream and 3rd Foot Guards, was part of the Allied force defending Cadiz and in 1811 the accoutrements and arms issued new in 1809 were still in use. The jackets of the Coldstream were said to be 'very short in the waist . . . and not very well fitted . . . First Guards also rather short in waist and wear the clothes of last year.' Their caps were also in poor condition, and when a supply of new ones was ordered, only 102 arrived. When the siege of Cadiz was raised the Guards marched to Seville, then on to Talavera, and reached Madrid before retiring to Salamanca – a total of some 640 miles. They then took part in the retreat to Portugal. One shudders to imagine their appearance after the rigours of a campaign first in the blistering Andalucian sun, then across the plains of León, and finally in torrential rain and mud during the retreat to Portugal.

While not strictly a matter of campaign dress, the question of billeting does bear directly upon the hardship of the men's appearance. Getting a good billet was always a preoccupation for officers in the Peninsula, and in this they were at the mercy of the Quartermaster General's Department. Quartermasters would ride ahead of the column, arriving in advance in the next town or village, where they would allocate certain streets or districts to certain battalions. They would select the best houses for senior officers, the next best for junior officers in order of rank, marking the doors with chalk. Houses allocated to the rank and file were marked with the number of men to be accommodated.

Many Guards officers brought tents to the Peninsula, or bought them on arrival; Rous paid 15 guineas for one at an auction, probably of the effects of a dead officer. It was not until March 1813 that tents were made standard issue, at a scale of one for each field officer, one for the company officers, one for the adjutant, quartermaster, medical staff and paymaster, and three per company for the NCOs and men – on the calculation that a proportion of men would always be absent on guard and other duties. (Officers continued to purchase their own tents, nevertheless.) When the demands of campaigning

benighted the army in the open, then officers and men alike did the best they could with cloaks and greatcoats, and rudimentary shelters of branches and blankets. Many was the night that the sons of earls and ploughmen shivered together in the frozen mud.

The Waterloo campaign opened in dramatic circumstances, with Foot Guards officers dashing away from the Duke of Richmond's ball to rejoin their battalions, and such was the speed with which the army assembled and marched off to Quatre Bras that many officers found their uniforms packed up and the baggage already strung out along the road; as a result many of them had to fight in their evening dress. Indeed, there was little time to wash or shave: when Captain George Bowles of the Coldstream wrote to Lord Fitzharris on 19 June, he said he had not washed his face or taken off his boots since the 16th. Two days after the battle, when the Guards were on the road to Paris, the order to halt was given and every officer and soldier set to work getting rid of the beards that had grown over the last few days. Ensign Gronow of the 1st Foot Guards relates that this task quickly sparked off the sporting instincts of the Guards officers when Lord Saltoun bet a fellow officer, Bob Ellison, that he could not shave off his beard in one minute – Ellison won the wager.

Other ranks' brass shoulder belt plate, 3rd Foot Guards.

The 2nd Battalion Coldstream Guards had sent six companies to Holland in November 1813, being joined in Brussels the following year by a further four companies. They were still stationed there at the outbreak of the Waterloo campaign. The battalion had received an issue of new clothing in 1814, but the 1st and 3rd Foot Guards were still wearing their 1813 issue in May 1815. By then the men's clothing was in poor condition, particularly the greatcoats, which prompted the Quartermaster of the Coldstream to write, 'We shall be very fortunate if they will hang on the men's backs two months longer. It is impossible to make them last near the summer. Many of the men have got them very much patched already.' By early May 1815 the much-needed new clothing for all four battalions of Guards had still not been packed ready for transportation to Brussels. The Quartermasters of the Coldstream had every confidence in being able to supply their 2nd battalion before hostilities broke out, but by 5 June the ships had still not sailed and it was not until the last day of July that the clothing finally arrived. The Guards certainly cut fine figures in Paris during the occupation; but on 18 June they defeated Napoleon's last army wearing the old, patched clothing issued a year – and in some cases, two years – before.

Officer's gilt gorget, Coldstream Guards, c.1810. The Royal coat of arms on the front with the regimental badge on either side. The rosettes are dark blue.

One final note concerns the condition of the 1st Foot Guards shortly after their return from Corunna in 1809. The battalion was stationed at Chatham, Kent, and was inspected in May 1809. It was noted that the men had recovered from the effects of the campaign and had been issued with new arms and clothing; the only defect occurred in their knapsacks. Apparently, the painter employed to paint the new packs, presumably of the Trotter pattern, used a composition of tar and turpentine, which evidently made a mess of them; he was accordingly ordered to paint them all again, which of course delayed their issue. It is interesting to note that upon their being issued with new equipment, the old accoutrements which were still fit to be used were issued to the Regiment's 3rd Battalion, although this latter unit was much in want of canteens and haversacks. It was at this time that the composite battalion of the Guards, which served under Dilkes at Barrosa, was being prepared for departure. The men's clothing and equipment were said to be in good order, but the inspecting officer noted that the flints were not very good, and mentioned the fact that the chapes of the bayonet scabbards were too short.

COLOURS

The colours of an infantry regiment were its most precious possession, serving not only as a rallying point in battle but also as the symbol which embodied the pride and spirit of the regiment. To lose one's colours to the enemy was as great a disaster as a regiment could suffer. The colours were placed in the front rank between the 4th and 5th Companies, and were guarded in battle by a number of sergeants (or colour sergeants, from 1813). British infantry colours measured 6 feet 6 inches wide by 6 feet deep, mounted on a pike 9 feet 10 inches long with a brass finial and a metal ferrule. In a strong wind they required some strength to hold upright, the more so since the ensigns carrying them were generally fairly young men; and in battle a large part of the colour was often rolled around the pike.

The death of Lieutenant-Colonel William Miller, 1st Foot Guards, at the Battle of Quatre Bras, 16 June 1815. Miller insisted on touching the colour one last time before he died. The two private soldiers wear oilskin covers over their shakos. Lithograph by Ackermann after Atkinson.

The King's Colour

Each regiment of the Foot Guards had three crimson King's Colours: the Colonel's Colour; the Lieutenant-Colonel's Colour; and the Major's Colour.

1st Foot Guards

Colonel's Colour: Crimson, with the Imperial crown in the centre.

Lieutenant-Colonel's Colour: Crimson, with a small Union flag in the upper canton.

Major's Colour: Crimson, as Lieutenant-Colonel's, but with gold blaze or 'pile wavy' issuing from the Union flag.

Coldstream Guards

Colonel's Colour: Crimson, with the Star of the Garter in the centre and the Imperial crown above.

Lieutenant-Colonel's Colour: Crimson, the same design as the Colonel's Colour, but with the Union flag in the upper canton.

Major's Colour: Same design as the Colonel's Colour, but with a Union flag in the upper canton, with a gold 'pile wavy' issuing from its lower corner.

3rd Foot Guards

Colonel's Colour: Crimson, with a red rampant lion of Scotland in the centre on a yellow shield, with the motto 'En Ferus Hostis' below and the Imperial crown above.

Lieutenant-Colonel's Colour: Crimson, with a red and white rose in the centre with a thorn issuing from one stem with the motto 'Unita Fortior' below and the crown above; it also has a small Union flag in the dexter canton.

Major's Colour: Crimson, bearing the Star of the Order of the Thistle with the motto 'Semper Paratus' and a small Union flag in the dexter canton.

The Regimental Colour

The Regimental Colour was the national flag. Each company of a Foot Guards regiment had a Company or Regimental Colour, distinguished by its own

Richard Simkin's painting of the 1st Foot Guards Trooping the Colour in 1814. The privates of the Battalion Companies turn out in full dress uniform of white pantaloons and gaiters, while the bearskinned Grenadier Company files into position in front of them. The NCO and privates of the Grenadier Company appear to dwarf those behind them: the average height of the company in 1809 was in fact 5 feet 11 inches, compared to 5 feet 7 inches in the Battalion Companies.

1st Foot Guards, officer's gorget, 1815, bearing the Royal coat of arms in the centre.

company badge, and one of these was borne in rotation by each battalion. By the time of the Waterloo campaign in 1815 the 1st Foot Guards had 24 company badges, the Coldstream 16, and the 3rd Foot Guards thirteen. The badges were as follows:

1st Foot Guards, Company Badges

1st: The Royal Crest in gold, a crowned lion standing on a large crown. *2nd:* A red rose surmounted by a white rose. *3rd:* A gold fleur-de-lys. *4th:* A gold portcullis with hanging chains. *5th:* A silver rose in a flaming sun. *6th:* A thistle in full colours. *7th:* A silver stringed gold harp. *8th:* A red-winged Welsh dragon on a green mount. *9th:* A silver greyhound with a red collar on a green mount. *10th:* The flaming sun. *11th:* A silver unicorn with a prince's coronet and a chain. *12th:* A white antelope with a ducal crown and chain standing on a green mount. *13th:* A white hart, gorged with a ducal crown and chain, on a green mount. *14th:* A white falcon with wings extended, perched on the barrel of a closed golden fetterlock. *15th:* A red rose with green stalks and leaves. *16th:* A white swan with extended wings, gorged with a ducal crown and chain on a green mount. *17th:* A white falcon with a sceptre standing on a tree trunk with red and white roses sprouting from the tree's right side. *18th:* A trunk of a tree with three leaves sprouting. *19th:* A golden sceptre and sword proper. *20th:* A crowned head in a tree on a green mount. *21st:* A sun rising behind clouds. *22nd:* A beacon or cresset with flames. *23rd:* Silver ostrich feathers, crossed. *24th:* A white hart with golden antlers springing from the gate of a golden triple-towered castle.

Coldstream Guards, Company Badges

1st: A white lion on a green mount, surmounted by an imperial crown. *2nd:* Three ostrich feathers with the motto 'Ich Dien'. *3rd:* A white and black spotted panther, having flames of fire coming from its mouth, on a green mount. *4th:* Crossed swords, with points upwards, in silver, the hilt and pommel in gold. *5th:* The St George and Dragon. *6th:* A red rose with golden seeds and green thorns in a garter. *7th:* A centaur provided with a bow and arrow on a green mount. *8th:* Two crossed sceptres in gold. *9th:* The knot of the collar of the Order of the Garter. *10th:* A carbuncle in gold. *11th:* A white boar, with gold tusks and hackle facing the pike on a green mount. *12th:* A

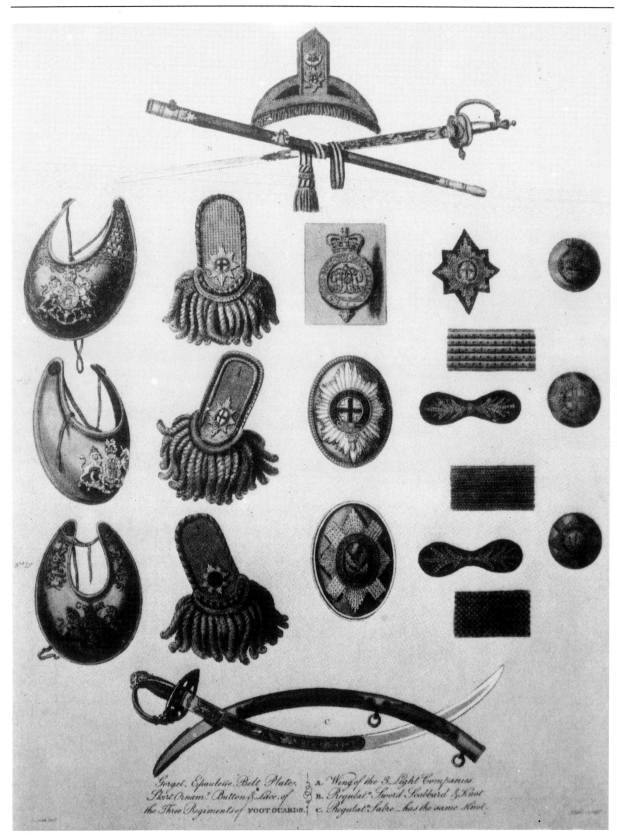

Gorget, Epaulette, Belt Plate,
Skirt Ornam.ᵗ Button & Lace, of
the Three Regiments of FOOT GUARDS.

A. *Wing of the 3 Light Companies*
B. *Regulat.ᵗ Sword Scabbard & Knot*
C. *Regulat.ᵗ Sabre—has the same Knot*

A plate, published in 1808, showing the various insignia, lace, badges, etc., of the three regiments of Foot Guards.

dun cow on a green mount. *13th:* A red and white rose impaled with a golden pomegranate bearing green leaves. *14th:* A white horse galloping on a green mount. *15th:* The crown of Charlemagne in gold. *16th:* Three crests of German origin, emanating from Saxony, Brunswick and Hanover.

3rd Foot Guards, Company Badges

1st: A red lion standing on an imperial crown all on a silver shield, with the motto 'In Defensio' beneath. *2nd:* A hand grenade with a lighted fuse. Motto 'Terrorem Affero' beneath. *3rd:* The red rampant lion of Scotland, with the motto 'Intrepidus' beneath. *4th:* The cross with a representation of St Andrew, upon a star of silver, all under a thistle. Motto 'Nemo Me Impune Laccesit' beneath. *5th:* A red lion passant and full faced, on a gold shield with the motto 'Timere Nescius' beneath. *6th:* A blue griffin on a gold shield, with the motto 'Belloque Ferox' beneath. *7th:* A phoenix rising from flames on a green mount, with the motto 'Per Funera Vitam' beneath. *8th:* A thunderbolt with silver wings, with the motto 'Horror Ubique' beneath. *9th:* A cannon represented as though in the act of firing a shot. Motto 'Concussae Cadent Urbes' beneath. *10th:* A salamander standing amidst flames, with the motto 'Pascua Nota Mihi' beneath. *11th:* A cross of St Andrew on a blue shield. Motto 'In Hoc Signo Vinces' beneath. *12th:* A trophy of arms, with the motto 'Honore Praefero' beneath. *13th:* A Talbot passant on a green mount, all in a gold shield, with the motto 'Intaminata Fide' beneath.

Battle honours

The first battle honours awarded to the 1st Foot Guards were granted in 1811: 'Lincelles' was awarded in June, and 'Corunna' and 'Barrosa' in October. Both these battle honours appear to have been added to the colours in 1814. After the Egyptian campaign of 1801 the Coldstream Guards were awarded the battle honour 'Egypt' and a Sphinx was added to the colours. The Sphinx was silver, and was mounted on a plinth inscribed with Egyptian heiroglyphics within a circular wreath of golden laurels with red berries; between the tips of the wreath was the word 'Egypt' in gold Roman capitals. The battle honour 'Egypt' was ordered to be painted on the Regiment's colours in 1807, but new colours were issued before this was done; it is not clear, therefore, when 'Egypt' was actually added to the colours, although it was present in 1811. On 20 June 1811 the Coldstream Guards were awarded the battle honour 'Lincelles', and on 12 February 1812 the honours 'Talavera' and 'Barrosa'. These were painted on to the colours in 1814. Like the Coldstream, the 3rd Foot Guards added a Sphinx to their colours after 1802, 'Lincelles' was awarded in June 1811, and 'Talavera' and 'Barrosa' in February 1812. These honours were added to all the Regiment's colours in 1814.

One final note concerns the battle honour 'Peninsula'. This was awarded in April 1815 and it is therefore rather doubtful whether it appeared on the colours of any of the regiments of Foot Guards at Waterloo. It certainly did not appear on the colours of the 1st Foot Guards, as the Major's Colour of the 3rd Battalion have only 'Lincelles', 'Corunna' and 'Barrosa'. The 2nd Battalions of the 1st, Coldstream and 3rd Foot Guards being stationed in Holland when the battle honour was awarded, it is probable that none of their colours carried at Waterloo bore the honour 'Peninsula', in spite of its being pictured in some much later paintings, notably Simkin's.

Other ranks' pouch badge, 1st Foot Guards, 1815.

ORGANISATION

At the beginning of the Peninsular War the 1st Foot Guards consisted of three battalions, the Coldstream and 3rd Foot Guards having just two. The organisation of each of these battalions was the same as for ordinary Line battalions, a system based on the 1792 *Rules and Regulations for the Formations, Field Exercise, and Movements of His Majesty's Forces* written by Colonel (later General Sir) David Dundas. Each battalion consisted of ten companies; one Grenadier, one Light, and eight Battalion. In theory, each company numbered about 100 men, giving a full-strength battalion a complement of 1,000 men. According to Dundas's *Rules*, each of these companies comprised 'four grand divisions; eight companies or platoons; sixteen sub-divisions; thirty-two sections, when sufficiently strong to be so divided.' This last phrase was a pertinent observation, for Wellington's battalions in the Peninsula were rarely up to anything like full-strength, only the Guards and a few of the better Line regiments ever being able to field a full-strength battalion. The table below gives the strengths of the Guards in seven major battles between 1808 and 1815; these figures show that the Guards were able to field an average battalion strength of 981. The average battalion strength of the Line regiments in the Peninsula was 550, but only in 1812, when the 1st Foot Guards were suffering severely from sickness, did a battalion of the Guards fall this low, numbering around 600 at this time.

Each battalion was commanded by a lieutenant-

A grenadier of the 1st Foot Guards, 1815. In spite of the grey service overalls bearskins were not worn on campaign.

The Strength of the Guards 1808–1815

Battle	battalion	strength*	battalion	strength
Corunna	1/1st Guards	1,361*	2/1st Guards	1,113
Talavera	1/Coldstream	970	1/3rd Guards	1,019
Busaco	1/Coldstream	814	1/3rd Guards	817
Fuentes de Oñoro	1/Coldstream	940	1/3rd Guards	959
Salamanca	1/Coldstream	954	1/3rd Guards	961
Nivelle	1/1st Guards	885	3/1st Guards	795
	1/Coldstream	918	1/3rd Guards	1,124
Waterloo	2/1st Guards	976	3/1st Guards	1,021
	2/Coldstream	1,003	2/3rd Guards	1,061

* These figures represent battalion strengths at the outset of the campaign. No accurate figures are available for strengths during battle.

Sergeant, private and officer of a Battalion Company, 1st Foot Guards, 1815. The officer's crimson sash was much wider than depicted in this painting by Simkin. The private's shako has white worsted cotton chain and tassels, the sergeant has gold cords, and the officer gold chain cord and tassels. Note the private's pricker and brush, attached to his jacket through his crossbelts.

colonel. There were also two majors per battalion; ten captains, one to each company; and 20 subalterns, half of them being ensigns and the others being lieutenant-captains. These lieutenant-captains were the result of a peculiarity of the Guards known as 'double-ranking' whereby the officers of the Guards held both regimental and 'army ranks'. This dated back to 1687, when a captain in the Guards was ranked as a lieutenant-colonel, and to 1691, when lieutenants were ranked as captains. This privilege meant that a captain in the Guards could exchange into a Line regiment as a lieutenant-colonel – not that many did, however, in spite of the slow speed of promotion in the Guards. For example, in the 3rd Guards the shortest time in which an ensign of 1809 became a lieutenant was four years and seven months; and of the 75 ensigns in the Brigade of Guards in 1809, only 18 became lieutenants within five years. Virtually all promotions during the Peninsular campaign were by way of seniority, mainly caused by the deaths of officers in action, rather than by purchase.

Drill

According to Dundas's *Rules and Regulations*, the normal marching rate, known as the 'ordinary step', was 75 paces of 30 inch length. The 'quick step' was 108 paces, also of 30 inches each, used when deploying from column into line and vice versa; it was also used on the parade ground. The quickest step was primarily used for wheeling or making up time; this was at 120 paces per minute, each of 20 inch length. (For greater detail on movements and drill, see Bryan Fosten's *Wellington's Infantry 1*, Men-at-Arms 114.)

Weapons

The training of the Foot Guards, and all other infantry of the time, revolved around their weapons. In the case of the Foot Guards this was the Land Pattern musket. This had a 42 inch barrel, took a .75 calibre ball and weighed 10lb $4\frac{1}{2}$ ounces. A 39 inch barrelled version of the musket was issued to the Light Infantry in 1810 and was probably issued to the Light Companies of the Foot Guards.

It was a clumsy weapon to load and fire, but this could be achieved three times a minute by trained infantrymen. It was not a very accurate weapon – its effective range was about 300 yards – and any man

A Negro 'time beater' or cymbalist of the 1st Foot Guards, c.1815. Red jacket with gold stripes, white turnbacks edged gold and what appears to be the letter 'G' on turnback. Pointed gold lace loops on lapels, white sleeves with gold chevrons and stripes, blue collars and elbows edged gold, blue cuffs with pointed gold lace loops, blue epaulettes edged gold, white turban with red top edged gold, with maroon ball decoration at back. Loose white trousers. This sleeve pattern survived for at least 150 years – until the 1930s.

lucky enough to hit his target at over 100 yards could consider himself fortunate. However, the power of these muskets when fired *en masse* proved enough to drive the French from the Iberian Peninsula and to defeat Napoleon at Waterloo. Loading involved biting the rear end off a paper cartridge containing about eight drams of black powder and a ball. A small amount of powder was poured into the priming pan, which was then closed. The remainder was then emptied down the barrel, followed by the ball, which was rammed down with a ramrod, the empty cartridge paper being used as wadding. It was possible for a soldier to achieve a rate of five shots a minute by pouring the charge down the barrel and then banging the butt on the ground; the bullet was then rolled down without wadding or the aid of a ramrod. Although this 'jogging' achieved a quicker rate of fire, it was at the expense of accuracy, the loose ball rattling out on even less predictable a trajectory than usual. Also, if the musket was presented at anything less than horizontal the ball could simply roll back out of a clean barrel. The bayonet was triangular in section, 17 inches long and was carried in a black leather scabbard; it was fitted to the barrel by a four-inch socket.

Officers of Battalion and Grenadier Companies wore the 1796 pattern infantry sword; this had a straight blade measuring 32 inches, a brass knuckle-bow guard, a ball pommel and side shells, all gilded, and a grip bound with silver wire. It was carried in a black leather scabbard with brass mounts, either in a frog or on slings.

Officers of the Light Companies carried a curved sabre with a brass knuckle-bow guard and a lion's head pommel, again gilded; the scabbard was black leather with brass mounts. Guards NCOs wore swords with slightly curved blades, and brass knuckle-bow guards with the regimental badge set in front; the pommel took the form of a lion's head, and the grip was of white cord and brass wire.

Bibliography

Dawnay, Major Nicholas Payan, *The Standards, Guidons and Colours of the Household Division, 1660–1973* (Tunbridge Wells, 1975).
Fletcher, Ian (Ed), *A Guards Officer in the Peninsula: The Peninsular War letters of John Rous, Coldstream Guards, 1812–14* (Tunbridge Wells, 1992).
Fletcher, Ian, & Poulter, Ron, *Gentlemen's Sons: The Guards in the Peninsula and at Waterloo, 1808–15* (Tunbridge Wells, 1993).
Fosten, Bryan, *British Foot Guards at Waterloo* (New Malden).
Fosten, Bryan, *Wellington's Infantry, 1 & 2* (Osprey MAA 114 & 119).
Haythornthwaite, Philip, *British Infantry of the Napoleonic Wars* (London, 1987).
Lemonofides, Dino, *British Infantry Colours* (London, 1971).

THE PLATES

A: Departure for the Peninsula, 1808
A1: Private, 1st Battalion, 1st Foot Guards
A2: Officer, 1st Battalion, 1st Foot Guards
A3: Sergeant, 1st Battalion, 1st Foot Guards
This plate is based on De Loutherbourg's painting 'Embarkation of the 1st Foot Guards for Corunna at Ramsgate, 8th September 1808'. The 1st Battalion numbered 1,361 men of all ranks, and the 3rd Battalion 1,113. The private is wearing white breeches and black gaiters, although other privates in De Loutherbourg's painting are shown wearing loose white trousers buttoned at the sides. Most of the Guards wore trousers once they reached the Peninsula. The Guards were still wearing the brown canvas knapsack, with the regimental badge painted on it, not yet having adopted the black 'Trotter' knapsack. The sergeant is wearing dark grey trousers, also depicted in De Loutherbourg's painting, another variation of legwear. His crimson sash has a white stripe through it, denoting the 1st Foot Guards; by the time of Waterloo the sergeants of all three Guards regiments wore plain crimson sashes. Chevron rank distinctions had been introduced in 1802. Unlike the NCOs of ordinary Line regiments, whose chevrons were of white silk, Guards sergeants wore three chevrons of gold lace on blue cloth on their right arm. Corporals wore two white silk chevrons on blue cloth, also on their right arm. Only the sergeants of the Light Companies were armed with muskets, so this Battalion Company sergeant carries the nine-foot-long spontoon. Both the sergeant and private wear

the 1806-type shako, made of felt, which replaced the much heavier leather version.

B: The Retreat to Corunna, 1809
B1: Private, 1st Battalion, 1st Foot Guards
B2: Sergeant, 1st Battalion, 1st Foot Guards
B3: Officer, 1st Battalion, 1st Foot Guards

This plate shows the Guards on the retreat to Corunna in the terrible winter of 1808/09. Guards or not, the weather and bad roads paid scant regard to rank or social standing; and an eyewitness, a soldier of the 71st Regiment, recalled: 'The officers, in many points, suffered as much as the men. I have seen officers of the Guards, and others, worth thousands, with pieces of old blankets wrapped round their feet and legs; the men pointing at them, with a malicious satisfaction, saying, "There goes three thousand a year," or, "There goes the prodigal son, on his return to his father, cured of his wanderings." Even in the midst of all our sorrows, there was a bitterness of spirit, a savageness of wit, that made a jest of its own miseries.' The two battalions of the 1st Foot Guards,

A sergeant and corporal, Grenadier Company, 3rd Foot Guards, 1815. Both men wear white plumes in the shakos, signifying the Grenadier Company. The sergeant's chevrons were gold lace on a backing of dark blue cloth, although this is not clear in this picture; the corporal's, of white worsted lace, are also on dark blue cloth. After a print by Vernet.

nevertheless, were notable for maintaining their discipline and bearing.

The sergeant wears the regulation grey woollen greatcoat. A Horse Guards order of 27 October 1806 stated that NCO's greatcoats were to have collars and cuffs of the regimental facing colour, which in the case of the Guards was dark blue. It also stated that chevrons were to be worn on the right sleeve of the coat in the same way as those on the jacket and of the same colour, i.e. gold lace on dark blue cloth.

C: Talavera, 27–28 July 1809
C1: Sergeant, Battalion Company 3rd Foot Guards
C2: Officer, Battalion Company 3rd foot Guards
C3: Corporal, Battalion Company 3rd Foot Guards

The colours of any regiment were often the focus of fierce fighting and were an obvious target for enemy troops. The colours, both Regimental and King's, were carried into battle by ensigns, often very young officers (sometimes as young as 16 years old), and at 6 feet 6 inches wide by 6 feet deep they could be quite a handful, particularly in a strong wind; a large portion of the flag might be wrapped around the 9 foot 10 inch-long pike to make it easier to control. The Foot Guards were unique in that they had three King's Colours: a Colonel's, a Lieutenant-Colonel's and a Major's Colour. At Talavera the fighting around the colours of the 3rd Foot Guards was particularly hot, and two ensigns, Scott and Aitchison, were badly wounded carrying them. The colour shown here is the Colonel's Colour, of crimson, with a rampant red lion of Scotland on a yellow shield with the motto 'En Ferus Hostis' (Behold a Fierce Enemy) below and the Imperial Crown above. The sergeant helps defend the colour with his 9 foot-long spontoon with its $12\frac{3}{4}$ inch blade.

In a long, close action several sergeants might be killed in this post, and others might be sent from the companies to take their place.

An officer of the Coldstream Guards, 1808, after a painting by H. Edridge. This officer, wearing the long-skirted pre-1812 coat, is holding the straight-bladed 1796-pattern infantry officers' sword. The flimsiness of officers' boots can perhaps be gauged by the fine, supple-looking boots worn in this picture – apparently more suitable for riding than walking, according to Gronow.

D: Salamanca, 22 July 1812
D1: Private, Light Infantry Company Coldstream Guards
D2: Officer, Light Infantry Company Coldstream Guards
D3: Sergeant, Light Infantry Company Coldstream Guards

Both the Coldstream and 3rd Foot Guards were present at the Battle of Salamanca, which was later awarded to both regiments as a battle honour. However, only the Light Infantry Companies took

An ensign of the Coldstream Guards, c.1816. This young officer wears the uniform of the Light Company with a Waterloo medal, he is possibly Henry Gooch, who was with the company on 18 June 1815. The very broad gold lace is illustrated well here on the wings and lapels.

they wore the normal shako plate but with a bugle horn beneath the Royal Cypher and trophies.

E: Foraging in the Peninsula, 1812
E1: Corporal, Coldstream Guards, Undress
E2: Officer, Coldstream Guards, Undress
E3: Private, Coldstream Guards, Light Infantry Company

The corporal in this plate wears his short white single-breasted fatigue jacket, and his 'pork-pie' fatigue cap with its pompom on top. According to Ensign Gronow of the 1st Foot Guards, when Wellington's army entered the south of France at the end of 1813 an order was issued requiring the men to wear their regulation scarlet or red jackets whilst out on fatigues or on foraging expeditions. This was because troops wearing their white fatigue jackets for such duties had been mistaken for marauding Spaniards. This caused great alarm in the countryside, since Spanish troops often took indiscriminate revenge for the French occupation of their country once across the border. Indeed, when Wellington's army crossed the Pyrenees into southern France, most of the Spaniards were sent home to avoid stirring the local population to resist the Allied advance. The officer in the plate wears a wide-brimmed sun hat, and has a field glass around his neck. The Light Company private has been allowed to unbutton the neck of his jacket but he still wears his leather stock.

F: Peninsula, 1812
F1: The Honourable W. Dawson, 1st Foot Guards
F2: Daniel Mackinnon, Coldstream Guards
F3: The Honourable Orlando Bridgeman, 1st Foot Guards

In this plate we see the Honourable William Dawson of the 1st Foot Guards. He was one of the more flamboyant officers and carried with him an immense personal supply of hampers full of wine, liqueurs, hams, potted meat and other delicacies brought out from England. He also had his own cooks – said to be the best in the army – as well as a host of servants from Spain, Italy, Portugal and even France. Such was the magnificent table kept by Dawson that even Wellington dined with him. Dawson was much loved by his brother officers, but they appear to have taken advantage of his good nature, for his stay in the

part in the action, being detailed to occupy the village of Los Arapiles, an important 'hinge' upon which Wellington based his operations during the battle. There was fierce fighting in the village streets as the French tried to wrest it from the Guards, but they held on, and it remained in Allied hands throughout the day. The soldiers in this plate wear trousers made from locally produced cloth, usually of a dark brown colour. The battalion had received a new supply of clothing in March 1812, but by the time of the battle they had marched their shoes off and were again in want of clothing and equipment. The sergeant carries a musket, unlike his counterparts in the Grenadier and Battalion Companies, who carried a spontoon. He also wears his sergeant's chevrons on his right sleeve only. The Foot Guards also had their own type of shako plate; and instead of displaying a bugle horn alone, as was usually the case with Light Companies,

Peninsula was cut short after about a year: as a second son he had only a younger brother's fortune, so his debts became very considerable, and he was eventually forced to quit the Guards.

Dining with Dawson in this plate is perhaps the most celebrated Guards officer of them all, Daniel Mackinnon of the Coldstream. In between spells at home recruiting he served in the Peninsula with the 1st Battalion from 1810 to 1813, and in Holland in 1814. Mackinnon was later one of the defenders of Hougoumont, where he was badly wounded. Famous in the army for his sense of fun and practical jokes, he would amuse his comrades by climbing over the furniture of a room like a monkey. Mackinnon's most infamous escapade involved his impersonating the Duke of York, a lengthy charade which ended with him diving head first into a bowl of punch.

The third officer is the Honourable Orlando Bridgeman, a captain in the 1st Foot Guards, seen wearing a fine red silk cloak given to him by Mademoiselle de Casteja, the fiancée of a wounded French officer taken prisoner in Seville in August 1812, whom Bridgeman chivalrously agreed to help leave Madrid. He delivered her into the hands of friends who got her to France. As Bridgeman helped her onto her horse on the outskirts of Madrid she changed her black velvet jacket and red silk cloak for clothing more suited to her journey, giving them to Bridgeman as a token of her appreciation. The cloak can be seen today in the Guards Museum, London.

The red silk cloak worn by the Hon. Orlando Bridgeman, 1st Foot Guards, during the Peninsular War. Given to him by a Spanish lady who later married a French officer, the cloak can be seen today in the Guards Museum, London.

G: The Pyrenees, 1813
G1: Officer, 1st Foot Guards
G2: Officer, Coldstream Guards
G3: Officer, 3rd Foot Guards

By the time Wellington's army reached the Pyrenees in late 1813 his men had adopted all manner of clothing. Sandals made from cow-hide cut to shape were very popular, as were trousers made from locally produced brown cloth. The officer of the Coldstream in this plate wears such a pair of trousers, strengthened with leather at the bottoms. He also wears a blue boatcloak, one of the many items purchased privately and sent out from England; he is wearing his forage cap, and carries an umbrella. The officer of the 1st Foot Guards wears the 1812-pattern shako, a headdress generally worn only by drafts of rankers arriving in the Peninsula towards the end of the war; but a number of officers had the new pattern specially sent out from England. John Rous of the Coldstream asked for the new-pattern shako 'with gold binding'; and a portrait of Sir Henry Sullivan of the same regiment shows this shako complete with gold binding around the false front, though this was probably removed on active service. The officer also wears his grey, calf-length, woollen overcoat, with a long cape reaching almost to the elbow.

H: Musicians
H1: Drum Major, 3rd Foot Guards
H2: Bugler, 3rd Foot Guards
H3: Drummer, 3rd Foot Guards

Among the bands of the Guards regiments usually only the drummers, buglers and drum major went on active service. The Guards did have a band in Paris after the Waterloo campaign, but there is no record of

Officer's shako plate, 1812,
Coldstream Guards. The
plate is gilt, with a silver
Garter Star and a red
enamel cross; the strap
and motto are gilt with
blue enamel backing.

I2: Private, Grenadier Company, 1st Foot
Guards
I3: Officer, Grenadier Company, 1st Foot
Guards

Nowhere was the splendour of the Foot Guards more in evidence than on State occasions such as the Trooping of the Colour, and while on guard duty at St James's Palace or Windsor Castle; and there was no more impressive uniform than that of the Grenadiers of the Foot Guards in their immaculate full dress. It was on these occasions that the Grenadier Companies wore their bearskins, although more than a few artists have, over the years, erroneously pictured the Guards as wearing them in battle. They were, however, taken on campaign: a return from the Guards at Barrosa states that many of the grenadiers were much in want of new bearskins or were without them altogether. The officer wears his splendid full dress coat with its broad gold lace. A white silk stock was worn with full dress; white gaiters and breeches were also worn by officers and men.

J: The Waterloo Ball, 15 June 1815
J1: Officer, Battalion Company, 1st Foot
Guards, Full Dress
J2: Officer, Grenadier Company, 3rd Foot
Guards, Full Dress
J3: Officer, Light Infantry Company,
Coldstream Guards, Undress

The Duchess of Richmond's famous Ball, set against the dramatic backdrop of Napoleon's swift move against the Allied armies of Wellington and Blücher, turned what was a regular occurrence for Wellington's officers into an occasion of almost legendary proportions. The ball gave the officers of Wellington's army a chance – and for many, their last chance – to don their finest uniforms and strut the ballroom in all their glory in front of some of the prettiest women in society. When orders for a general concentration were suddenly issued many officers found their baggage packed and were forced to march and fight the next day at Quatre Bras in the full dress uniforms worn at the ball the previous evening. Ensign Gronow of the 1st Foot Guards certainly did, while others fought with grey overalls hastily pulled over their evening dress. The officer of the 1st Foot Guards wears his full dress uniform, which shows off the extensive gold lace decoration around the

them having actually served during the campaign itself. Other band musicians included cymbalists and serpent players, the former often being Negroes, who were prone to leap about and dance as they played. The drum was of course the method by which most commands were relayed to troops, the company drummers often beating frantically to be heard above the din of battle. The bugles of the period were made of copper with a brass rim, and green cords signified the Light Company, which had buglers instead of drummers. The musicians in this plate wear their service dress. A much more lavish uniform was worn by bandsmen on State occasions which included 'jockey caps' and gold-laced coats.

I: 1st Foot Guards, St James's Palace
I1: Sergeant, Grenadier Company, 1st Foot
Guard

pockets. The 1802 dress regulations stated that Light Infantry officers should wear a long-tailed coat for full dress, with silver bugles on the tails, although this Coldstream officer wears his undress jacket, an alternative often worn by officers of Light Companies. He is also carrying a 'chapeau bras', a smaller version of the cocked hat which was often worn on such occasions. The Captain of the 3rd Foot Guards wears his epaulettes over his Grenadier Company wings.

The coat worn by Lieutenant-Colonel William Miller, 1st Foot Guards. Note the regimental star on the turnbacks and the thin dark blue edging to the broad gold lace.

K: Hougoumont, 18 June 1815
K1: Officer, Coldstream Guards
K2: Pioneer, Coldstream Guards
K3: Private, Coldstream Guards

The successful defence of the château of Hougoumont by the Foot Guards proved to be one of the decisive factors in Wellington's victory at Waterloo. The château was initially defended by the four Light Companies of Foot Guards present at the battle, although the two Light Companies of the 1st Foot Guards (two battalions were present) subsequently withdrew to join their respective battalions with the main Allied line on the ridge behind Hougoumont. The defence was then entrusted to the 3rd Foot Guards and all but two companies of the Coldstream. The château had begun to be turned into a defensive position by the Pioneers as soon as they had occupied

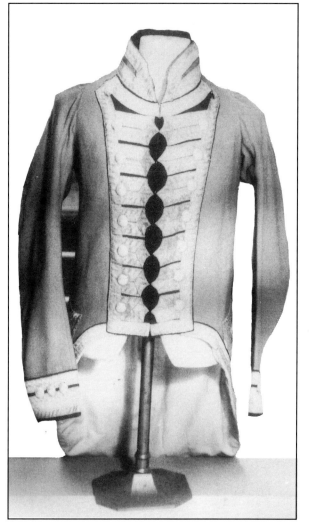

the place on the night of 17 June; firesteps were constructed, loopholes pierced and barricades erected. Although the French hurled entire divisions at the place on the 18th, they were thrown back by the tenacious defenders. Only once did the French succeed in entering the courtyard when they forced open the North Gate, but this was closed soon afterwards and every Frenchman inside, bar one drummer boy, put to the sword.

The Pioneer in this plate, a corporal, wears a leather apron and is sporting the distinctive Pioneer's beard; he carries an axe and in his belt has a billhook, a popular tool used throughout Wellington's army. Pioneers were also armed with muskets, although this particular man does not carry his. Pioneers wore their trousers tucked into their gaiters. Note also the black tape ties on the shakos of the Coldstream officer and private, as shown clearly by Dighton in his painting of the defence of Hougoumont.

L: Waterloo, 1815
L1: Colour Sergeant Charles Wood, 3rd Battalion, 1st Foot Guards

During the afternoon of Waterloo the 1st Foot Guards found themselves attacked not only by the French 105th Infantry Regiment, but also by enemy artillery that raked their lines with canister and horsenails. The 3rd Battalion took the brunt of the attack, with frightful wounds being suffered by the men. It was 'the hottest part of the contest', wrote Colour Sergeant Wood of the 3rd Battalion, who added that he feared the men would not stand. It was at this point that he stepped forward and picked up the bloodstained jacket worn by Ensign Purdo of the same battalion, who had been killed earlier in the afternoon; Purdo had been stripped by plunderers and his body lay across a dead horse. Picking up the jacket, Wood stepped about 25 paces in front of the line and waved it in the air, cheering his comrades and shouting, 'While our officers bleed we should not reckon our lives dear!' Wood also mentioned the fact that the carnage from enemy fire was so great that file upon file was carried to the rear wounded, and that the Guards' line was getting eight or ten deep in places. This forced the sergeants to prop up the line

William Miller's full dress uniform; note the very broad gold lace on the scarlet collar and on the dark blue cuffs. The coat is lined with white silk.

by placing their spontoons across the backs of the men to steady it. Wood was one of only two colour sergeants left standing after the battle, and later stood by the King's Colour 'from the moment of our march, till borne, in Britain's name, within the gates of Paris'. The rank of colour sergeant was instigated by Royal Warrant dated 27 July 1813, the colour sergeants of the Guards receiving pay of 2s 6d per day. While the Coldstream and 3rd Foot Guards wore white trousers during the campaign, the 1st Foot Guards appear to have worn grey service trousers tucked inside their gaiters.

This miniature shows an officer, apparently of the 1st Foot Guards, who has been identified as regimental staff, possibly an assistant surgeon. He wears an epaulette bearing the Star of the Order of the Garter on a scarlet jacket with dark blue collars edged gold.

Notes sur les planches en couleur

A Inspiré de la toile de De Loutherbourg qui décrit ce régiment s'embarquant pour le Portugal. Différents types de pantalons sont représentés dont de larges pantalons blancs, des culottes blanches portées avec des guêtres, des pantalons gris comme celui que porte le sergent sont également dépeints sur cette toile. Les soldats portent le shako de feutre de 1806 qui avait récemment remplacé le modèle en cuir épais. La musette en toile marron est encore utilisée. La rayure blanche sur la ceinture du sergent caractérisait ce régiment à ses débuts. En 1815 les sergents de la Garde portaient tous une ceinture pourpre unie. Les sergents de la Garde étaient différenciés par des chevrons de dentelle dorée pour indiquer leur rang.

B Des témoins ont décrit le délabrement de l'armée durant sa retraite vers Corunna.

Farbtafeln

A Aufbruch des Regiments nach Portugal, dem Gemälde von De Loutherbourg nachempfunden. Die Männer tragen unterschiedliche Hosen, einige weitgeschnittene, weiße Hosen, andere weiße Reithosen mit Gamaschen; graue Hosen, wie sie der Sergeant trägt, sind auch auf dem Gemälde zu sehen. Die Soldaten tragen den 1806er Tschako aus Filz, der seit kurzem den schwereren aus Leder ersetzte. Der braune Ranzen aus Segeltuch wird noch verwendet. Beim weißen Streifen auf der Schärpe des Sergeanten handelt es sich um ein frühes Regimentsabzeichen; bis zum Jahr 1815 trugen die Sergeanten des Garderegiments alle einfarbig karminrote Schärpen. Die Sergeanten des Garderegiments waren durch goldene Rangwinkel gekennzeichnet.

Beaucoup marchaient pieds nus car les chaussures bon marché avec lesquelles ils étaient équipés s'étaient désintégrées mais la discipline et la conduite supérieures de la Garde étaient bien différentes de l'effondrement d'autres régiments. Les grands pardessus des sergents avaient un revers de col et de poignets de la couleur de leur régiment c'est-à-dire bleu foncé pour la Garde à pied et des chevrons sur la manche droite seulement.

C A Talavera il y eut de sévères combats autour des enseignes du 3ème régiment de la Garde à pied: l'enseigne du Colonel, portée comme un drapeau du roi, est illustrée ici. Deux jeunes enseignes furent blessés en la défendant, ainsi que plusieurs sergents. On leur demanda de défendre les enseignes dans toutes les batailles avec leurs piques de 9 pieds et dans une bataille sanglante les sergents étaient quelquefois détachés de plusieurs compagnies et envoyés progressivement pour remplacer les blessés à ce poste honorable mais dangereux.

D La Garde Coldstream, que l'on distinguait par des boutons et de la dentelle regroupés par paires, portait sans doute un pantalon marron fabriqué sur place durant cette campagne. La Compagnie légère portait un écusson de shako spécial et ses sergents, qui avaient des chevrons sur le bras droit seulement, portaient des mousquets plutôt que des piques. Les officiers des Companies légères portaient diverses distinctions dont de courtes vestes et imitaient souvent le style d'équipement de la cavalerie légère. Les Coldstream prirent part à d'âpres combats dans le village de Los Arapiles à Salamanque.

E Le caporal porte la veste et la casquette blanches de corvée, la première comportant des revers colorés en partie et la seconde comportant le pompon rouge du Bataillon ou Companies centrales. L'officier porte un large chapeau de soleil et un téléscope en bandoulière. Les officiers en campagne portaient en grande partie ce qu'ils voulaient.

F Scène de détente. Les trois officiers représentés, tous des personnages bien connus dans la Péninsule, sont inspires de portraits. Dawson, un hôte très généreux, négociait toujours l'emploi de muletiers supplémentaires pour ses énormes quantités de bagages. Mackinnon, un homme plein d'humour qui aimait les plaisanteries et les exploits physiques extraordinaires, fut par la suite gravement blessé à Hougoumont. Bridgeman reçut ce manteau de soie rouge des mains d'une dame espagnole, fiancée à un officier français blessé qu'il aida à s'échapper.

G L'officier des Coldstream porte un calot, un manteau bleu et un pantalon fabriqué sur place renforcé de cuir. L'officier du 1er régiment de la Garde à pied porte le nouveau shako de 1812, une rareté dans la Péninsule mais porté à la fin de la campagne par les nouvelles recrues anglaises (et, dans la Garde, avec un passepoil doré à l'avant) par certains officiers qui les avaient demandés. Notez le pardessus de l'officier avec sa longue cape.

H Tambours de la compagnie. Dans les Compagnies légères, les clairons faisaient partie des effectifs normaux d'un bataillon et transmettaient les ordres durant les batailles. L'orchestre était un organisme indépendant, non officiel et généralement employé et payé par les officiers eux-mêmes. Le tambour major était généralement le seul membre à prendre un service actif. Dans une bataille statique, les musiciens prenaient souvent le rôle d'aides infirmiers et aidaient les blessés à se rendre jusqu'au chirurgien sur les arrières.

I La splendeur de l'uniforme officiel complet tel qu'il était porté pour les occasions officielles à Londres. On dit que les compagnies de Grenadiers avaient emmené leurs chapeaux à poils en campagne car plusieurs documents en parlent, mais ils n'étaient jamais portés durant le service actif car on les gardait en sécurité pour les parades. Les hommes de la compagnie portaient le shako comme leurs camarades. L'uniforme officiel avait une culotte et des guêtres blanches et des chaussettes blanches également.

J Au bal légendaire donné par la Duchesse de Richmond le 15 juin 1815 à Bruxelles, les jeunes hommes des Guards profitèrent d'une magnifique soirée en compagnie des dames de la société. Beaucoup d'entre eux furent appelés d'urgence pour se battre à Quatre Bras dès leur sortie du bal et certains se battirent en bas et chaussures de danse. Certains moururent même dans ce costume. Un officier ici, J3, d'une Compagnie légère, suit la mode de son unité en portant sa veste de petite tenue plutôt que le manteau d'apparat richement paré de dentelle. Remarquez le capitaine de Grenadiers, 3ème régiment de la Garde à pied, que l'on distingue par ses deux épaulettes situées sur les 'ailes' de sa compagnie.

K La défense de Hougoumont par la Garde Coldstream fut l'un des moments épiques de Waterloo. Le Pionnier qui avait aidé à fortifier le château la nuit précédente en construisant des gradins de tir, en crénelant les murs et en montant des barricades, se reconnaît par son tablier de cuir, sa barbe et ses outils. Les détails des autres uniformes viennent de la toile de Dighton qui décrit cette bataille et qui est très spécifique quant aux uniformes.

L Durant l'après-midi de Waterloo le 1er régiment de la Garde à pied fut violemment attaqué et le 3ème bataillon perdit énormément d'hommes à cause de la proximité du feu des français. L'artillerie utilisait en effet de la mitraille et des clous à ferrer. Le sergent chef Charles Wood, voyant ses hommes hésiter, sortit seul des rangs et ramassa la veste ensanglantée de l'enseigne Purdo, dont le corps se trouvait entre les deux armées, dénudé par des pillards. En agitant cette veste au dessus de sa tête, il ramena ses soldats à leur devoir. A la différence des Coldstream et du 3ème régiment de la Garde à pied, il semble que le 1er régiment à Waterloo portait un pantalon gris rentré dans les guêtres.

B In Berichten von Augenzeugen wird der schäbige Zustand der Armee auf dem Rückzug nach Corunna beschrieben. Viele Männer gingen barfuß, nachdem die billigen, ausgegebenen Schuhe kaputtgegangen waren; doch herrschte bei den Garderegimentern im Gegensatz zu einigen anderen Regimentern erstaunliche Disziplin und gutes Betragen. Die Mäntel der Sergeanten hatten Krägen und Manschetten mit Blenden in den Regimentsfarben, d.h. dunkelblau für die Garderegimenter, und Rangwinkel nur auf dem rechten Ärmel.

C Bei der Schlacht von Talavera kam es zu heftigen Kämpfen um die Flagge des 3. Garderegiments; hier ist die Flagge des Oberst abgebildet, die als die Flagge des Königs getragen wurde. Bei der Verteidigung der Flagge wurden zwei junge Fähnriche und mehrere Sergeanten verwundet. Sie hatten in ihrer Stellung die Flagge mit ihren 2,75 m langen Piken im Kampf zu verteidigen. Bei blutigen Schlachten mußten oft Sergeanten mehrerer Kompanien herangezogen werden, um die wiederholten Opfer dieser ehrenhaften, doch gefährlichen Stellung zu ersetzen.

D Die Coldstream Guards, die an den Knöpfen und paarweise angeordneten Litzen erkenntlich waren, trugen auf diesem Feldzug wahrscheinlich vor Ort hergestellte, braune Hosen. Die Leichte Kompanie trug eine spezielle Tschakoplatte, und die Sergeanten, die ihre Rangwinkel nur auf dem rechten Arm trugen, hatten Musketen anstelle der Piken. Die Offiziere der Leichten Kompanien trugen verschiedene Kennzeichen und kurze Jacken und übernahmen oft den Ausrüstungsstil der leichten Kavallerie. Die Coldstream Guards wurden in der Ortschaft Los Arapiles in Salamanca in heftige Kämpfe verwickelt.

E Der Obergefreite trägt die weiße Arbeitsjacke und -mütze, erstere mit farblichen Blenden und letztere mit der roten Quaste des Bataillons beziehungsweise der Mittelkompanie. Der Offizier trägt einen breitkrempigen Sonnenhut und hat ein Teleskop umhängen; die Offiziere trugen im Feld weitgehend was sie wollten.

F Fröhliche Szene außer Dienst. Die drei abgebildeten Offiziere sind Porträts nachempfunden. Es handelt sich um auf der Pyrenäenhalbinsel wohl bekannte Persönlichkeiten. Dawson, ein überaus großzügiger Gastgeber, versuchte stets, zusätzliche Maultiertreiber auszuhandeln, so daß er eine große Menge Gepäck mitbringen konnte. Mackinnon, der stets zu Späßen aufgelegt war, gern Streiche spielte und Kraftproben vorführte, wurde später bei Hougoumont schwer verwundet. Bridgemans roter Seidenumhang war das Geschenk einer spanischen Dame, der Verlobten eines verwundeten französischen Offiziers, der er geholfen hatte, sich in Sicherheit zu bringen.

G Dieser Offizier der Coldstream Guards trägt ein Schiffchen, einen blauen Schiffsmantel und vor Ort hergestellte Hosen, die mit Leder verstärkt sind. Der Offizier des neuen 1812er Tschako, der auf der Pyrenäenhalbinsel selten war, jedoch gegen Ende des Feldzugs von neu eingezogenen Soldaten aus England getragen wurde, sowie – in den Garderegimentern mit goldenen Borten an der Vorderseite – von einigen Offizieren, die sich ihn von Zuhause schicken ließen. Man beachte den Mantel des Offiziers mit dem langen Cape.

H Kompanietrommler, wie sie bei den Leichten Kompanien Hornisten, gehörten zur normalen Bataillonsaufstellung und gaben bei Schlachten Befehle weiter. Das Musikkorps war eine separate Körperschaft, es war inoffiziell und wurde für gewöhnlich von den Offizieren angeheuert und aus eigener Tasche bezahlt. Der Tambourmajor war normalerweise das einzige Mitglied, das aktiven Dienst tat. In statischen Gefechten fungierten die Musiker oft als Lazaretthelfen und halfen den Verwundeten zum Arzt in der Nachhut.

I Die prächtige Paradeuniform, wie sie bei öffentlichen Pflichten in London getragen wurde. Die Grenadierkompanien nahmen ihre Bärenfellmützen wahrscheinlich mit ins Feld, da sie in verschiedenen Unterlagen erwähnt werden; doch wurden sie nie im aktiven Dienst getragen, sondern für Paraden aufbewahrt. Die Männer der Kompanie trugen Tschakos wie ihre Kameraden. Zur Paradeuniform gehörten weiße Reithosen und Gamaschen und weiße Strehkragen.

J Auf dem legendären Ball, der am 15. Juni 1815 von der Herzogin von Richmond in Brüssel gegeben wurde, amüsierten sich die jungen Herren der Garde mit den Damen der Gesellschaft. Viele wurden dringend zum Dienst bei Quatre Bas direkt aus dem Ballsall gerufen, und einige kämpften in Strümpfen und Tanzschuhen; einige starben sogar in diesem Aufzug. Ein Offizier einer Leichten Kompanie, hier J3, folgt der Mode seiner Einheit und trägt seine Interimsuniform anstatt der reich verbrämten Paradejacke. Man beachte den Hauptmann der Grenadiere, 3. Garderegiment, der sich durch zwei Epauletten auszeichnet, die über den Abzeichen seiner Anschlußkompanie getragen werden.

K Die Verteidigung von Hougoumont seitens der Coldstream Guards war eine der Heldentaten von Waterloo. Der Pionier, der in der Nacht zuvor bei der Befestigung des Schlosses geholfen hatte, Ausfallstufen und Schießscharten gebaut und Barrikaden errichtet hatte, ist an seinem Lederschurz, dem Bart und dem Werkzeug erkenntlich. Die Merkmale der anderen Uniformen stammen aus Dightons Gemälde der Schlacht, das die Uniformen genau darstellt.

L Am Nachmittag der Schlacht von Waterloo wurde das 1. Garderegiment heftig angegriffen, und das 3. Bataillon erlitt im Nahkampf mit den Franzosen, deren Artillerie es unter anderem mit Kartätschen und Hufnägeln beschoß, schwere Verluste. Der Oberfeldwebel Charles Wood sah wie seine Männer zauderten, schritt alleine von den Rängen und hob die blutige Jacke des toten Fähnrichs Purdo auf, der entblößt und geplündert zwischen den Armeen lag. Er schwenkte die Jacke über seinen Kopf und rief somit seine Soldaten zu ihrer Pflicht. Im Gegensatz zu den Coldstream Guards und dem 3. Garderegiment scheint das 1. Regiment bei Waterloo graue Hosen getragen zu haben, die in die Gamaschen gesteckt wurden.